Key to shells displayed on front endpaper

1 Pecten albicans
Japan

2 Chlamys nipponensis
Japan

3 Chlamys ventricosus
Peru and Ecuador

4 Chlamys ventricosus
Peru and Ecuador

5 Chlamys asperrima
Australia

6 Chlamys (Aequipecten) pallium
South East Asia

7 Chlamys (Aequipecten) townsendi
West Pakistan

8 Chlamys varia
Atlantic coast of Europe

9 Chlamys islandicus
Northern Europe and North America

10 Amusium japonicum
Japan

11 Mimachlamys australis
South West Australia

THE SCALLOP

THE SCALLOP

Studies of a shell
and its influences on humankind

by

eight authors

EDITED BY IAN COX, C.B.E., M.A.

PUBLISHED IN LONDON BY THE 'SHELL' TRANSPORT

AND TRADING COMPANY, LIMITED

1957

Design and production adviser Charles Rosner

Made in Great Britain

CONTENTS

FOREWORD

On 18 October 1957, The 'Shell' Transport and Trading Company, Limited will celebrate the sixtieth year of its existence. A Diamond Jubilee, marking as it does the passing of two generations, cannot but give pause for reflection on the changes and progress that time has wrought; but few industries can look back on so great a metamorphosis and such vast expansion as has taken place in the oil industry during these sixty years. In these tremendous developments, Shell, I am proud to say, has been at all times in the forefront.

Ten years ago, on the occasion of the Company's Golden Jubilee, the story of Shell's progress and expansion was the subject of a booklet which, in the exigencies of that time, could be but a brief and modest publication. It is, therefore, with all the greater pleasure that I now introduce this book to mark the occasion of the Company's Diamond Jubilee.

In the chapters which follow, each by a distinguished author on the topic he has chosen, there are revealed some of the lesser-known aspects of the story of the scallop shell, of its uses in ancient times, as a symbol in heraldry, in art and architecture, and of its association from early times with pilgrimages to Spain. From these pleasant incursions into the past, our authors lead us to the important place which the scallop holds today in the gastronomic arts.

The preface to a book of this nature would, I feel, be incomplete without some reference to the reasons which inspired Marcus Samuel, who with his brother Samuel Samuel founded our Company and became its first Chairman, to select a shell as the Company's badge and title. There can be no doubt that he drew his inspiration from the ornaments decorated with sea-shells which were sold by his father, Marcus the elder, in Victorian days.

The sea-shell which the brothers Samuel adopted as a symbol of their new and growing business (and which they registered as their trademark) was not the scallop shell as we know it now, but a shell of somewhat indeterminate appearance, and it was only in May 1904 that the orthodox scallop shell became the Company's trademark.

The scallop had figured in the affairs of man from the earliest times, but its use was declining when it was adopted as the title of the Company and emblem of its trade, so we can properly claim to have given this ageless symbol a new life and a new significance. Its adoption has thus a certain romance in itself and its application to the products with which we are associated has undoubtedly played a highly important part in the Company's great development.

The fact that some of our competitors in the international oil industry subsequently followed our example by adopting one emblem world-wide is not without significance.

In concluding this foreword, I think I may say that our shareholders and our staff, no less than the public, have come to regard our shell as a sign of the highest industrial integrity of one of the world's greatest trading enterprises.

Chairman

SHELL:

A WORD'S PEDIGREE

B. Woledge

The Great Scallop.

WHEN we hear the word 'scallop' today, it may suggest to us a shell, or a piece of embroidery, or something to eat, while the word 'shell' may call to mind eggs, snails, petrol, shelling peas, or shelling enemy positions. Turning to what etymologists have discovered about the history of these words, we find ourselves considering such widely different events as the spread of the Germanic tribes over the Roman Empire, the Viking settlement in Britain, and the expansion of modern Western civilization.

It is sometimes difficult enough to find the origin of words that spring up during our own lifetime (for example, no one is sure of the origin of 'gremlin' or 'O.K.') and older words can hardly ever be traced right back to their origins, far beyond the short period for which we have written records to help us. However, an enormous amount of work has been done by etymologists during the last hundred and fifty years, and their comparisons of related words surviving in different languages and dialects make it possible to reconstruct the prehistory of words and follow their changes and wanderings with a good deal of precision. Thanks to their work, we now know, for example, that 'scallop' and 'shell' are so closely related to each other as to be, in a sense, merely different forms of the same word.

Some centuries before Christ, the Germanic tribes inhabiting Central Europe had a word that is the ancestor of 'scallop' and 'shell'; it consisted of the sounds *SKAL* followed by various endings, and it conveyed the idea of some sort of hard covering, but we shall never know how it got this meaning, or whether it was first used for the covering of a crab, a snail, an egg, or a nut. The peoples who used this word – Saxons, Goths, Franks, and the others – were restless and energetic. During the third to sixth centuries A.D., after the Romans had proved unable to keep them back, these tribes wandered over most of Europe, and spilt into Asia and Africa as well. Wherever they went, the syllable *SKAL* with its appropriate endings doubtless went too; and speakers could make use of it not only in traditional ways, but also to describe various kinds of hard coverings that were new to them – new either because they developed them in their own culture or because they came across them in lands where they had not lived before: coverings of dwellings, large shells used as plates or cups, peapods, shells of tortoises, scales of snakes. Man does not need a new word every time he invents or meets a new thing; it is often handier to use a familiar word, giving it a slight twist in meaning: electric *bulb*, dust *bowl*, air *hostess*.

Young Queen Scallops at the stage when they are anchored by byssus threads.

The earliest written evidence we have of the existence of *SKAL* is in the Gothic translation of the New Testament, which was made in the fourth century on the shores of the Black Sea; the word is here used for tiles in the passage that is familiar to us as 'they went upon the housetop and let him down through the *tiling* with his couch into the midst before Jesus'. With the passage of time, written examples accumulate, and *SKAL* can be seen giving rise in different languages to a whole group of different words and meanings, far too many to be mentioned here.

When Hengist and Horsa landed in Kent about the year 449, they certainly were in the habit of using words of the *SKAL* group, and wherever Angles, Saxons, or Jutes evicted the Celtic inhabitants from their lands, hard coverings came to have names of this kind. Anglo-Saxon literature has preserved for us, in manuscripts from the tenth century onwards, words of this group in several dialects. By far the most important is the word we now pronounce 'shell'. (It was the habit of the Anglo-Saxons to turn *SK* into *SH*, while the Danes who followed them kept to the traditional *SK*. So we have 'shirt' and 'skirt', two forms of the same word.) Incidentally, the Danes brought their own version of the old *SKAL*, which we still use whenever we speak of a pair of scales, for the meaning of the word had shifted from 'shell' to 'shell used as container' and hence it could apply to various sorts of container. Long after the word 'scale' had passed from the Danes to the English, in fact until about a hundred and fifty years ago, a scale was a bowl as well as a weighing instrument.

Meanwhile, in what we now call the Netherlands, another group of Germanic wanderers had settled with their words of the *SKAL* family, which are still in use today: the modern

12

Young Queen Scallop anchored to a branching marine animal.

Dutch words for 'shell' and 'rind' are *schil, schel, schelp*. It is the last of these three which has become '*escalope*' in French and 'scallop' in English.

To the medieval Frenchman '*schelp*' (or '*scelpe*' as it was then) was not an easy word to pronounce, but we often adopt foreign words in spite of pronunciation difficulties: we make a shot at '*embonpoint*' and '*hors d'œuvre*' and sometimes turn '*café*' into 'cafe'. The main reason why the French found '*scelpe*' hard to say was that they were not used to clusters of consonants like *SK* and *LP*; they got over the difficulty by putting in extra vowels (just as today Italians get over similar difficulties in English), and so turned '*scelpe*' into '*escalope*' and '*escalipe*'. Why the French took this word from abroad is a mystery so far unsolved. They may have heard it from Dutch pilgrims wearing the scallop as an emblem, or perhaps the fishermen of northern France picked it up from their Dutch neighbours. Whatever the reason for adopting the word, the French made good use of it in the Middle Ages, applying it to shell-fish, to snail shells and to nut shells; it was not yet used, however, as it is now, for a slice of veal served in a special way.

The later history of this word in France is curious, for it almost disappeared from use for about three hundred years. Its later re-emergence and subsequent glory are due to the genius of some *chef de cuisine* who, probably in the 1830's, baptized his new way of serving veal '*escalope de veau*'. We do not know either where he found the word or why he chose it; it may have come from his own local patois, but why call a slice of meat a scallop? It is for the historian of French cooking to give us the answer.

In the Middle Ages, when *escalope* still meant 'shell', it was natural enough that it should

13

cross the Channel. From 1066 till the fourteenth century the language of the English royal family and of a large part of the nobility was French, and many people in the south of England were constantly switching from one language to the other and mixing the two. So the old French word '*escalope*' was frequently heard in Norman England; English people mispronounced it as 'scallop' and it is mostly in this form that we know it today, although we still have the alternative 'escallop', mainly used in heraldry.

Once acclimatized, the word proved extremely useful in England, and a glance at the various uses recorded in the Oxford English Dictionary reminds us how adaptable words are, or rather how ingenious human beings are in adapting old words to new uses.

We notice first that the word became specialized: it ceased to be applied to snails or nuts, and was restricted to one particular shape of shell. This narrower, more precise meaning then became the starting point for fresh applications: it was the mollusc that lives in the shell; a vessel resembling a scallop shell (used in baptism); a pilgrim's badge; an ornament on the edge of a garment shaped like a scallop shell, and a collar having an edge of that kind. Another line of development was to use the noun as a verb: to scallop is either to shape the edge of a garment or to ornament with scallops, or to bake (oysters, etc.) in a scallop shell. The Oxford Dictionary also records a less common word 'scalloper' meaning one who makes scalloped edgings or who gathers scallops. Such a multiplication in the uses of a word is extremely common in many languages, perhaps in all, and it would take a long time to catalogue the various meanings of 'shell' in English or of '*coquille*' in French. The link between the different meanings is usually clear, but there are exceptions, and we see little resemblance between a sea-shell and a high-explosive shell, or between '*coquille*' meaning 'cockle' and the same word meaning 'misprint'. As it happens, the artillery shell was the name of the empty case before it was used of the complete object, explosives and all; as for '*coquille*' meaning misprint, it has so far defied all efforts to unravel its history.

We have traced 'scallop' and its related words from the forests of prehistoric Germany to the England and France of today. The story would not be complete if we did not also remember how modern civilization has carried these words from Western Europe all over the globe. The expansion of the last four hundred years has in fact been as dramatic as the tribal wanderings of earlier centuries. Whereas in 1500 these words were almost entirely confined to Western Europe, they are now to be heard in one form or another in every continent; no doubt 'shell', the shortest and simplest of the *SKAL* words, has the largest currency of any member of the family, but 'scallop' is used wherever English is fully known, and '*escalope*' is used, not only in all French-speaking parts of the world, but wherever French cooking is appreciated.

It has truly been said that etymology, the study of words, is merely one aspect of the history of mankind and his culture; other aspects of the same theme are developed severally by the distinguished authors of the chapters that follow.

THE

LIVING SCALLOP

W. J. Rees

The Great Scallop, seen at low tide, South Devon.

THE scallop is a mollusc, a member of a very large group of animals which includes the oysters, the whelks, the octopuses, and the slugs. It belongs to the bivalves, a subgroup which is distinguished by having a pair of shells but, unlike its rather inactive relatives, the scallop is a very lively creature, for it has regained some of the lost mobility of its race, and can, in fact, swim in its own inimitable fashion. This evolution of a swimming habit makes it a particularly interesting animal to the biologist.

'Scallop' is a general term which can be applied to nearly three hundred different species living in warm and temperate seas the world over. They all conform to the general pattern we associate with the name – an almost round outline with ribs radiating like a Roman comb, which is why Pliny called them *Pecten*. Nevertheless, within this general pattern, the different kinds are sufficiently distinct from each other to be regarded as different species; indeed, no two kinds ever have exactly the same niche in Nature. In the fossil record *Pecten* has existed as a recognizable genus for about 150 million years. Some geologists go even further and trace its descent from *Aviculopecten*, remains of which occur in rocks 300 million years old.

We do not even have to choose a particular species for study, for the choice – the shell of St James – has already been made for us centuries ago. This emblem of the pilgrims to the apostle's tomb at Compostela in north-western Spain has long been known to the French as *Coquille Saint Jacques*. The only true *Pecten* which occurs on the Atlantic coast not many miles from Compostela is *P. maximus* – the great scallop. This, then, is the true St James's shell (a conclusion borne out by its representation on the vestments of the apostle, a subject to which Christopher Hohler gives his attention in a later chapter), but this is not to say that some of its close relatives are not, on occasion, employed in its stead. At Compostela itself even, a smaller and somewhat less symmetrical scallop, known to the fishermen locally as *Zamboriña*, and to the biologist as *Chlamys opercularis*, has come in for official use. The local name of the true St James's shell is *Vieira*. Both of these occur also in British waters; the larger we call the scallop and the smaller (*Chlamys*) is known as a 'queen' in the south and a 'clam' in Scotland.

The scientific naming of animals follows an established system which allows alteration in the light of newer knowledge. The great scallop is no exception; it was first called *Ostrea*

17

maxima by the great Swedish naturalist Linnaeus in the days when many bivalve shells were grouped with the oysters. In 1776, Otto Müller, a Dane, saw the need to distinguish the scallops from the oysters, a family to which they are indeed but remotely related, and following Pliny he called them *Pecten*. The St James's shell then, became *Pecten maximus*. It is interesting, however, that another species of scallop, very similar to it, lives in the Mediterranean. This too was known to Linnaeus but, strangely enough, he gave it the name of *Ostrea Jacobaea*. Why he did this, when it is *Pecten maximus* and not the southern species that lives on the coast of Galicia where the legend of St James is rooted, is a mystery. Is it possible that he thought that Compostela, and Padron where the body of the apostle was brought ashore, were on the Mediterranean coast of Spain, or was he influenced by the fact that the Crusaders also wore a *Pecten* shell as a badge?

Since the days of Otto Müller, the genus *Pecten* has itself been subdivided on account of various differences between its members, and nowadays there are many of these pectinids, obviously enough scallops of one kind or another, which no longer carry the name. The end papers of this book illustrate a few of them. However, I think we need only consider one of these allied species in detail. The close studies that have been made both on its life history and habits throw considerable light on the nature of the great scallop to which it is so very similar. This is the *Chlamys* (erstwhile *Pecten*) *opercularis* which I have already mentioned as the *Zamborina* of north-west Spain and as the 'queen' or 'clam' in Britain. Its more obvious differences from the great scallop are that it has two convex valves, instead of one convex and one flat, and one of its 'ears' is markedly larger than the other. It is, too, slightly smaller and, because of its lighter weight, the better swimmer.

Scallops are gregarious creatures. They sometimes congregate in thousands on favoured beds of clean firm sand, and they occur in small numbers almost anywhere where the bottom is suitable between depths of 60 and 500 ft. Occasionally they are found in special localities, like the Salcombe Estuary in South Devon, at low water during spring tides. The very young are absent from the commercial beds but they are sometimes found on the shore at low water or in pools. David Landsborough, the Scottish naturalist, writing about the Ayrshire coast, noted 'the fry of *Pecten opercularis* skipping quite nimbly through the pool. Their motion was rapid and zigzag, very like that of ducks in a sunny blink rejoicing in the prospect of rain. They seemed, by the sudden opening and closing of their valves, to have the power of darting like an arrow through the water. One jerk carried them some yards, and then by another sudden jerk they were off in a moment on a different tack. We doubt not that, when full grown, they engage in similar movements, though, as Pectens of greater gravity, they choose to romp unseen and play their gambols in the deep.' With growth the scallops move into deeper water, and when they are older they seem to undertake substantial migrations; this explains why they are not always found in the same place.

In appearance no other molluscan shells have so pleasing a design and range of colours as pecten shells, and it is small wonder that they have stimulated man's imagination all over the world since the earliest times. In the great scallop the right valve is flat and slightly overlapped by the left one which is convex. At rest on the sea bottom the flat valve is uppermost.

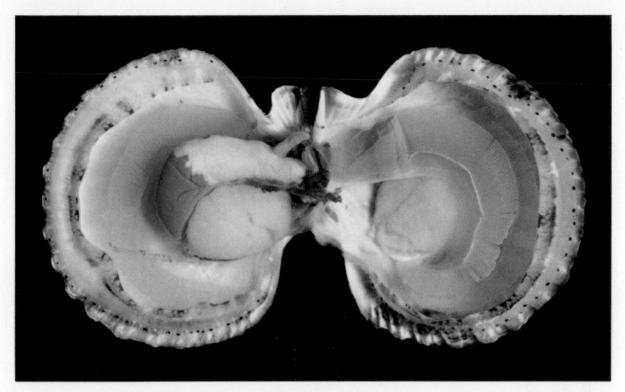

The Queen Scallop when freshly opened.

The two valves are held together along the hinge line by an external ligament; inside there is a triangular shaped elastic ligament which acts very much as a piece of india-rubber would if it were put in the hinge of a door: it becomes compressed when the valves are closed by the pull of the muscle between them and, when this muscle is relaxed, it expands again and causes the valves to gape.

The shell itself is brittle and much lighter in weight than in sedentary bivalves of similar size. Typically there are fifteen to sixteen ribs radiating from the central hinge line in each valve; these alternate with grooves and give the scallop its comb-like appearance. The so-called 'ears' are extensions of the hinge line. New growth is added all round the margins of the valves by a special band of secreting cells along the edge of the mantle – a soft 'jacket' that envelopes the entire animal within its shell. The beautiful colours that characterize all pectens are laid down when the shell is being formed. It is suspected that these may be due to the deposition of unwanted pigments acquired during digestion. This is known to take place, for example, in dog whelks whose shells acquire a blue colour when they have been feeding on mussels.

In life, the scallop (in this instance the queen) has been described by Philip Henry Gosse, the father in Edmund Gosse's *Father and Son*, in words that I cannot better: 'Its ordinary condition is to lie with its valves separated to a distance of about one-sixth of an inch. The open space is occupied by what seems a fleshy cushion, extending from one valve to the other

19

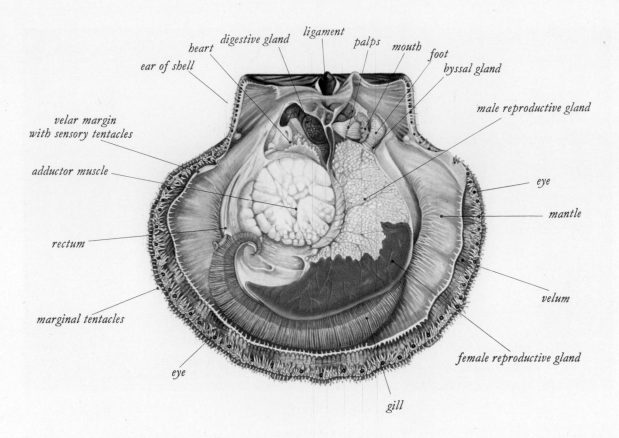

The labels in the illustration, reading around the figure:

ear of shell · heart · digestive gland · ligament · palps · mouth · foot · byssal gland · male reproductive gland · velar margin with sensory tentacles · adductor muscle · rectum · marginal tentacles · eye · gill · female reproductive gland · velum · mantle · eye

The Great Scallop opened to show what lies within the shell. The right (flat) valve has been removed and with it the right half of the mantle and the right gill.

all round, but just within its edge. It is of a delicate flesh-colour, with mottlings of dark brown, making a kind of irregular pattern with transverse bands; a close examination, however, shews that this substance is divided into two parts. This is, in fact, *the mantle*, of which these two parts are the thick and glandular edges. Around its circumference, on each portion, just where it is in contact with the valve, there are set a great number of tentacles – delicate thread-like organs, tapering to a fine point, and of a pellucid white appearance; they are capable of being protruded and retracted at the will of the animal. . . . Frequently the animal protrudes them to their utmost extent, bending them back above the edges of the shell, and waving them slowly in every direction.

'But the most beautiful feature of this animal is yet to be described. In the line of the larger tentacles, and alternating with them, is seen a row of minute circular points, of high refractive power, possessing all the brilliancy of precious stones. They look indeed like diamonds of the first water, each set in a ring or socket of black substance, which greatly enhances their beauty. They are about half as numerous again as the radiating grooves of the shell; but are not set with perfect regularity. They are still less uniform in size, some having a diameter twice as great as others. These are believed to be eyes, and certainly they are well placed for enabling the animal to watch the world around it. It is very sensitive, withdrawing its

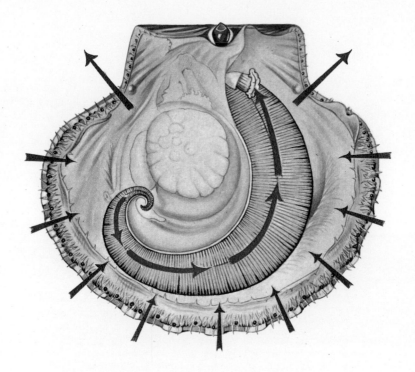

Breathing and feeding: the blue arrows indicate the direction of the water currents bringing in oxygen and food; the red arrows show the passage of food particles, filtered by the gills towards the mouth.

tentacles and mantle, and bringing the valves of its shell together, on any shock being given to the vessel in which it is kept. I observed, however, that it will not actually close the valves, unless it is repeatedly disturbed, or unless the shock be violent; contenting itself with narrowing the opening to the smallest space appreciable; even then the two rows of gem-like eyes are distinctly visible, peering out from the almost closed shell; the two appearing like one undulating row from the closeness of their contiguity. A friend, to whom I showed it when nearly closed, compared them not unaptly to a lady's ring set with small brilliants.'

If you wish to see the structure and relations of its different internal organs, you should lay the scallop on its flat valve and remove the convex valve by cutting through the adductor muscle and breaking it away at the hinge line. This will entail removing the right half of the mantle, which is contiguous with the shell, and the left gill which looks like a flimsy folded net. The drawing at the top of the opposite page shows what is left.

In the centre is a large creamy white body. This, of course, is the adductor muscle which has already been cut across to separate the shells. Below it are the bright cream and orange-red reproductive glands, and below again is the delicate crescent-shaped gill. Fringing the edge of the shell is the curtain-like edge of the left half of the mantle, with its tentacles and iridescent eyes. Between the adductor muscle and the hinge lies the dark green or almost

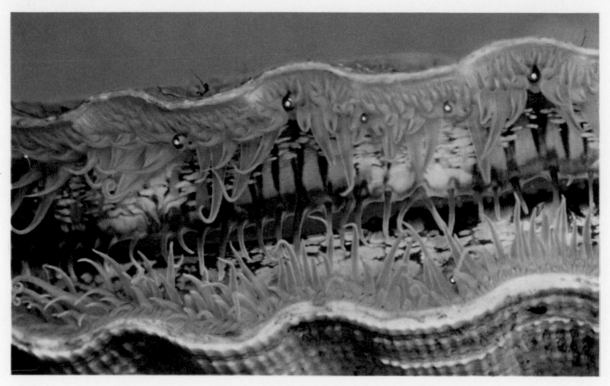

The mantle edge of the Queen Scallop seen between the gaping valves. Enlarged.

black mass of the digestive gland, and to the right of it in the picture are the labia or lips of the mouth and the small 'foot', which is less important in the adult than in the young, as we shall see presently. The course of the alimentary canal (as it winds through the digestive gland, the reproductive organs, and doubles back passing above the adductor muscle) cannot be seen for it is embedded in tissue; it opens just behind the adductor. When the scallop is prepared for the table the foot, the mantle, and the gills (often collectively termed the 'beard') are discarded together with the digestive gland (called the 'black mark' in the older recipes).

The scallop is rich in sense organs and of these the eyes around the mantle margin are the highest developed. Additionally, however, there are numerous small sensory cells scattered all over the skin, but especially on the tentacles at the margin of the mantle. In the living animal, these tentacles can be protruded and they are in constant motion. Equipped with these cells they behave like an advance guard and give warning of danger; even a slight disturbance in the water is enough to make them contract quickly.

The drawing of the open scallop on page 20 shows a fold of the mantle margin called the velum. Here there are guard tentacles of a different kind, which, when the scallop's valves gape, form a screen through which food and water are drawn in. These tentacles seem to have a sense of smell; at any rate they are sensitive to minute chemical changes in the seawater. This was established by experiments carried out with a species of scallop on the Atlantic coast of the United States. It was found there that when crushed parts of a starfish

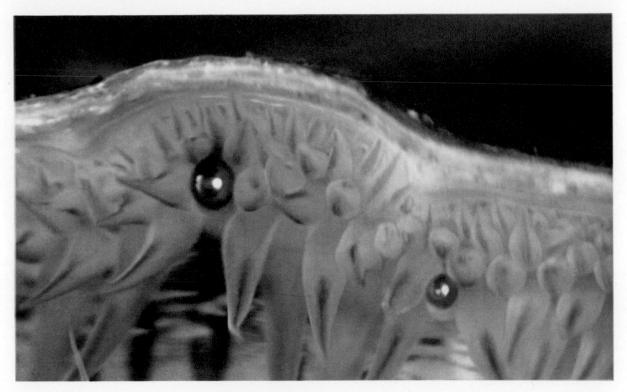

The mantle edge of the Queen Scallop much enlarged to show the eyes.

(its principal enemy) were brought near the velar tentacles, the scallop firmly and quickly closed its valves. Tentacles on other parts of the mantle, however, showed no response.

The eyes of *Pecten*, on which I have already quoted Gosse, may number up to a hundred in a large animal and they are well formed. Each has a lens, a retina, and an optic nerve. They are unquestionably better developed than in any other bivalves, but we still have a good deal to learn about them. It is, for instance, doubtful if they can perceive images at all clearly but they are particularly sensitive to light. If, for example, the shadow of an object, moved in front of the shell, falls on the eyes, then the valves close immediately. They can also perceive movement whether or not it involves a change in brightness; they will react by shutting their valves when, say, a small white card only three-fifths inches square is moved against a black background more than a foot away.

The gills of the scallop are exceptionally important because they create the water currents which bring in food and the oxygen necessary for life. As well as this, they provide a selective filter for the food particles (mostly microscopic plants) and convey them towards the mouth. Structurally, the gills are curtains made up of filaments between which water can pass. Each one of the pair is folded in the form of a W. The cells of which the filaments are composed have microscopic 'hairs' called cilia projecting from the surface. These, in their myriads, beat in the water and create a current which enters the scallop between the velar tentacles, passes through the gills (where the food particles are trapped in mucus) and out of the shell on either side near the ears. Other cilia carry the food-laden mucus to the

Capture and demise: I - The common starfish with its arms around the scallop.
II - With the suction of its tube feet, the starfish pulls the valves apart.

III-The starfish extrudes its stomach around the soft parts of the scallop.
IV-The starfish, viewed from below, with a small scallop in its stomach.

lower edges of the gills and thence to the mouth. The routine is illustrated in the simplified diagram at the top of page 21.

Occasionally if the gills receive too much food, or if the water is heavily laden with silt, the gill can discard the mucus strings into the mantle cavity. The mantle, too, is ciliated and all foreign particles are carried to strategic points near the exhalant apertures where they are expelled into the water. Sometimes the gill may be partly smothered with particles; it can then execute a writhing movement to free itself. Accumulations within the mantle cavity can be quickly expelled during swimming.

Most scallops have concentric rings on the shell and by counting the number of these it is possible to tell their approximate age. Allowance must be made, however, for the period prior to sexual maturity (about two to three years) when no rings are formed. Growth in the great scallop, as indicated by the distance apart of the first three rings, is rapid, but after this it slows down progressively, so that beyond the ten-ring stage the gaps between succeeding ones are often less than one millimetre. Very little growth takes place after seventeen rings, although shells with twenty-two rings have been noted. In the Irish Sea it has been noticed that these rings are formed during a period of very little growth from April to June, in other words, cessation of growth corresponds to maximum spawning activity.

Within the pecten family some species have the sexes in separate individuals and others are hermaphrodite. Both the great scallop and the queen are hermaphrodite, but in *Pecten tenuicostata* of the American coast, for example, the sexes are separate. In the two species with which we are mainly concerned, the female reproductive glands are a bright orange red when ripe, while the male portions are creamy pink in colour. Apart from the creamy-white, round, adductor muscle, the reproductive glands are the most conspicuous features of the scallop as it lies dressed on the fishmonger's slab.

From researches made in the Isle of Man, it is known that the great scallop becomes sexually mature at two to three years old and, as is often the case in molluscs, the male part of the reproductive organs matures a little earlier than the female. Broadly speaking, spawning goes on from January to August, with a particularly active period in March; throughout these months there appears to be a spawning maximum at about the time of each full moon. The great scallop seems to require a sea temperature of at least 10°C. before it will spawn.

In *Chlamys opercularis* (the queen) the breeding season is from January to June inclusive. Here, too, there is some evidence that the ripening of sexual products comes at the time of full moon. Both for the scallop and the queen, therefore, the gourmet should select the first half of the year at the time of the full moon if he is to eat them at their best – that is, when they are richest in protein.

Not a great deal is known about the earliest stages of development of the scallop. In the case of the queen, the egg is round and about 0·068 mm in diameter when it is discharged into the water. It is then that it is fertilized and proceeds to develop into a larva. This is in contradistinction to many bivalves whose eggs are fertilized within the mantle cavity, which becomes a brood chamber for them. The queen's larva has a swimming membrane and a thin transparent shell and it lives at or near the surface for some days or weeks. Nothing

Escape from an enemy: I - The valves open widely as the starfish approaches.

further is known about its history, but if we are to judge from other kinds of scallop it eventually settles down on some hard object, loses its swimming membrane, and changes into a minute miniature of the adult.

At this stage the 'foot' is usually large enough to enable the shell to crawl to a suitable position for settlement. In moving, the foot extends, attaches its tip to the substratum and then contracts, drawing the body of the animal forward in successive movements until the desired position is reached. During this process the shell is poised over the foot with the hinge uppermost in much the same way as a snail carries its house.

Once the shell has found a suitable place to tarry while growing, the tip of its foot is closely pressed against the surface and then withdrawn. During this process a special kind of thread is secreted and firmly attached to the substratum. By repetition of this movement three or four of these threads (known collectively as byssus) are secreted to anchor the young shell, as seen on pages 12 and 13. In the scallop and the queen the byssus serves only for temporary attachment, the animals breaking away on reaching a certain size; but some of the other pectens (*Chlamys varius*, for instance) spend their whole life attached by byssus, in the same way as the edible mussel (*Mytilis edulis*) and the fan shell (*Pinna nobilis*). Others again, like the thorny 'oyster' (*Spondylus*) to which Adrian Digby refers in a later chapter, become cemented to the substratum for life and develop thick shells.

Once the byssal anchors break, either through the increased weight of the shell or by deliberate swimming movements, the scallop lies free on the bottom. In the great scallop,

Escape from an enemy: II - *The scallop propels itself upward in a flurry of sand.*
III - *The valves are now open as the scallop takes in more water preparatory to another dart.*

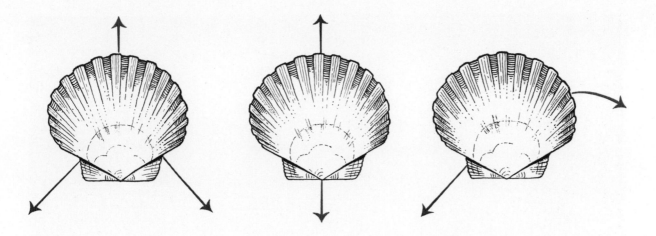

How the scallop swims. The blue arrows denote the propelling jets of water, the red the direction in which it moves. Above: forward swimming movements; below: the 'escape' movement.

the normal adult position is with the flat valve uppermost and the convex one beneath. Thus the opening of the shell is raised clear of the bottom, so that it can draw in the clearest water for breathing and feeding when it is at rest. When the animal is swimming normally this same position is maintained, but the free margins of the shell face forward and the hinge line backward. When, however, it has to execute the 'escape' movement, it goes in the opposite direction.

The chief enemy of the scallop is the starfish. As soon as one comes near, it will attempt an immediate escape by swimming. If the scallop is not quick enough, the starfish wraps its arms around it and, by exerting a continuous pull, eventually overcomes the resistance of the adductor muscle and forces the valves apart. It then extrudes its stomach and proceeds to ingest the soft parts from between the valves. This is well illustrated by Dr Wilson's remarkable series of photographs reproduced on pages 24 and 25. The whelk also feeds on scallops; apparently it gets the thin part of its shell between the valves and then attacks the adductor muscle with its proboscis. Sometimes, too, the scallop is attacked by a boring sponge (*Cliona celata*) which forms extensive ramifications through the shell and may, indeed, perforate it. When this happens the mantle seals off the ends of the tubes by secreting new shell in the form of black or grey nodules.

Hangers-on are sometimes a nuisance in the life of the scallop, for the flat upper valve offers an attractive anchorage for sedentary animals such as hydroids, barnacles, serpulid

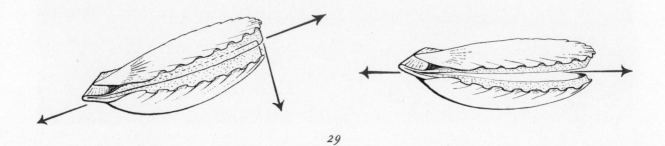

Escape from an enemy: IV- The lower scallop is about to close the margins of its mantle. V- The mantle margins are now closed, ready for jet propulsion.

Escape from an enemy: VI - The scallop returns to the sea-bed.

worms, sponges, polyzoans, and even large oarweeds. The weight of these hampers swimming, and may be formidable enough to ground the scallop permanently. When this is caused by long growths of weed, the shell can be said to be 'absalomed'.

Probably the most spectacular feature of the scallop is its prowess as a swimmer. Any sudden ejection of water from between its valves will cause it to move hinge foremost; but since the edges of the mantle are muscular and can form themselves into the nozzle of a jet anywhere around the margin, the scallop has considerable control over the direction it takes. There are, in fact, three distinct kinds of movement it can perform: normal swimming, twisting, and the so-called 'escape' movement. These are seen at their best in the queen, which is smaller and lighter, but the great scallop can also perform them and, in addition, has a characteristic fourth movement for righting its shell when it is overturned.

In the typical swimming movement speed depends on the vigorous clapping together of the shell valves and the associated strength of the jets of water which are expelled. As the animal prepares to swim, the valves open more widely than in the resting condition and the mantle curtains appear to be drawn inwards as if by water flowing in. Just as the valves of the shell reach their maximum gape, the mantle tentacles are suddenly retracted all round and the shell shuts with a snap. Simultaneous with this the mantle curtains become closely pressed together, preventing the escape of water except where they do not meet – that is, on either side of the hinge line. Thus, with the sudden closure of the shell, two jets of water are forced out between the ears and the scallop moves forward. Meantime some water escapes, to a lesser and controlled extent, around the free margins of the valves (where the upper curtain of the mantle can be adjusted to overlap the lower one) and so between them they produce a downward jet all round, which initiates the take-off from the bottom and maintains the upward movement of the shell. The animal then moves upwards and forwards in the direction of the free margins of its shell in an erratic motion which looks as though it were taking a series of bites out of the water as it claps its valves together. By a slight variation of this jet propulsion, the scallop can execute a somersaulting movement if it finds itself lying on the sand in an overturned position. By suitably adjusting its mantle curtains, it rights itself by suddenly expelling water downwards all round the free margins of the valves.

The 'escape' movement is used when the scallop is suddenly faced with a known and feared enemy, such as the starfish. Philip Gosse has observed this in the queen and his description is worth quoting: 'I perceived the lips of the mantle (which were held in contact, though the valves were considerably separated), suddenly open to a partial extent, *as if by a blowing from within*. At this instant there was a leap in the opposite direction, attended with a considerable agitation in the water. With this clue, I observed more definitely . . . The mode of proceeding is as follows: when the Pecten is about to leap, it draws in as much water as it can contain within the mantle, while the lips are held firmly in contact. At this instant, the united edges of the lips are slightly drawn inward, and this action gives sure warning of the coming leap. The moment after this is observed, the animal, doubtless by muscular contraction, exerts a strong force upon the contained water, while it relaxes the forced contact of the lips at any point of the circumference, according to its pleasure. The result is, the forcible ejection of a jet of water, *from that point*; which, by resilience of its impact upon the surrounding fluid, throws the animal *in the opposite direction*, with a force proportioned to that of the *jet d'eau*. The action may be well imitated by the human mouth blowing a stream of air from any determined point, while the lips are held firmly together at all other points. The resemblance, indeed, of the mantle to the human lips performing such an action (a resemblance perhaps more close than flattering) struck me as ludicrously faithful. Nor was the appearance less suggestive of a pair of bellows without a nose, of which the valves were the covers, and the mantle the leathers, discharging their contents from any part of their sides.' Thus, twisting movements can be executed by expelling water from different points along the edges of the mantle curtains; additionally, the animal can spin on its axis without leaving the bottom by discharging water at one point only.

The beauty of the scallop and of the mechanism that enables it to perform these movements are truly among the wonders of the natural world. In observing them, we cannot but feel as Gosse did in the year 1852 when he was watching the queen and was 'constrained to say with the Psalmist, *I will praise Thee; for (all is) fearfully and wonderfully made; marvellous are thy works, and that my soul knoweth right well!*'

A SYMBOL

IN ANCIENT TIMES

Sir Mortimer Wheeler

Ancestral altar in the courtyard of a Roman house, Herculaneum.

THE art of the classical world is strewn with scallop shells. Behind the gracious Aphrodite of Botticelli, borne lightly shoreward upon her Renaissance scallop, and behind the shell-hoods with which Queen Anne's architects enriched the porches of our London houses, are a myriad scallop motifs in Hellenistic and Roman terra-cotta, metalwork, painting, and carving. Their intent, whether symbolical or purely decorative, is often hard to assess, and may sometimes have been indifferently present to the minds of their users; but of the liking or habit which retained them in a variety of contexts through the classical and into the Byzantine world there is no manner of doubt.

Let us begin by recalling a few examples of these usages to illustrate their range. In the Hermitage Museum at Leningrad is an earthenware jug elaborately shaped and coloured to represent the head and shoulders of a young woman emerging from between the opening valves of a scallop shell, with pearls round her neck and breast and a garland about her hair. It was modelled by a Greek craftsman, probably about 400 B.C., and was found at Taman on the northern shores of the Black Sea. As a work of art it cannot be rated very highly, but it has the distinction of being perhaps the oldest example known of a long series of representations of the Birth of Aphrodite (Venus) from a shell. Its theme recurs a few years later on a two-handled jar found by the excavators of Olynthus, a town with a stormy history in the peninsula of Chalcidice at the northern end of the Aegean. This is shown on the following page. Between figures of Hermes and Poseidon, god of the sea, who are depicted in the russet red of the vase upon a black background, is a large white scallop shell behind which protrude the head and arms of Aphrodite with white flesh and golden hair. Poised beside her is Eros or Cupid, his wings outstretched and an arm extended towards her. Just as the goddess Athene was represented as born mature and armed from the head of Zeus, so Aphrodite is seemingly shown here as rising fully grown from the shell. The complication that Eros was recognized in ancient myth as a son of Aphrodite does not appear to have disturbed the artist in his rendering of the episode.

Nor did other artists hesitate to include Eros in the scene of his mother's birth. A charming terra-cotta from Corinth, now (or formerly) in the Berlin Antiquarium, shows Aphrodite kneeling between the open valves of a scallop shell, with a cloth, appropriately resembling a large bath towel, held under and behind her by a winged Eros. The relaxed figure of the

Burial urn: Olynthus, Greece.

goddess and her half-arrested, half-wondering gaze give this little work a quality above the average of its kind, and suggest derivation from some major sculpture now lost to us. But only second to it is yet another of the many Hellenistic representations of Aphrodite kneeling in the newly-opened shell; a terra-cotta probably from Greece but now in the Paris Louvre, illustrated on the next page. This shows a rather thickset *paysanne*, lacking the more delicate grace of the Berlin figurine but expressive of the small coloured terra-cottas which, as votive offerings or as traditional ornaments, enlivened the shops and shrines of Athens or Corinth in the third century B.C.

All this, however, is merely the beginning of our classical scallop shells. As a transition to the next group we may take a niche from Pompeii, richly adorned with mosaic decoration. In the semi-dome that forms the head of the niche the mosaic represents a scallop in which lies the figure of Aphrodite, whom we may now, in Italy of the first century A.D., call Venus. Another mosaic from the same famous site, overwhelmed by the volcanic ash of Vesuvius in A.D.79, shows Venus accompanied by Eros and a Triton (half man, half fish), who hold the shell between them. Details apart, the important innovation in these designs is the use of a scallop shell as the head of a niche – the remote ancestor of the Queen Anne shell-porch from which we started.

Now the earliest known example of this architectural use of the scallop motif is dated by an inscription to the year 87 B.C. It occurs in a grotto dedicated beside a spring to the rustic god Pan at Baniyas in Syria, and owes its architectural celebrity to the twin accident of survival and specific dedication. How much further back, and where, the niche-motif actually originated is unknown, but the chances are that it did not long precede the second century B.C. Its popularity seems to have spread quickly, and there are many examples of it at Pompeii and its contemporary neighbour Herculaneum. One is the subject of the plate on page 34. But it was by no means confined to the classical lands. Far away on the western fringe of the Empire, the scallop roofed the niches of deities who were sometimes strange to the Mediterranean world. Thus in 1646 a terrific storm upturned the dunes of the Island of Walcheren and laid bare the images, altars, and foundations of a curious Roman shrine, long since lost beneath the sea. It had been dedicated about A.D.200 to an otherwise unknown goddess Nehalennia, who is represented as a standing or seated matron within a scallop-headed niche keeping, as an inscription suggests, a protective eye upon cross-Channel trade with Britain.

The motif was already current in wall-painting before the destruction of Pompeii; and it was adopted on occasion also by the manufacturers of mosaic flooring, with special regard to the aptness of the design to the apsidal end of a room. In this fashion it was, for instance, used effectively, though with a certain bizarre freedom, in a house of the middle of the second century in the Roman city of Verulamium, twenty miles from London, as will be seen from the drawing on page 39. To what extent it was formally significant or purely decorative in all these various circumstances is a difficult matter which will be considered presently.

During the period of the Roman Empire, indeed, and particularly in its eastern half, the shell-niche was used on every type of monument. Notable examples are the marble

'The Birth of Aphrodite': Greek terra-cotta.

Mosaic floor from a house in the Roman city of Verulamium, St Albans. About A.D.150.

sarcophagi of the so-called 'Sidamara' series, which are thought to have been characteristic of Asia Minor and of the second to third century A.D. On the sides and ends of these distinctive sarcophagi the 'mourners' stand before or between niches with emphatic scallop shell heads (as shown on the next page) in a fashion which has suggested to one scholar the elaborate architectural façade of the classical theatre. And the arrangement survived, with variations, into the ivory carvings of the latest classical and post-classical age; for example, on the famous sixth-century throne of St Maximian at Ravenna, on which St John the Baptist and the four evangelists stand similarly in front of scalloped recesses.

In other ways, too, the scallop is associated with Roman funerary monuments. Particularly is it used as a sort of shield or medallion behind the portrait-bust of the dead man or his wife (or both). With this function it appears on the stone cists which contained the ashes during the prevalence of cremation in the first two centuries of our era. Sometimes it crowns the gravestone, free-standing; more often it is placed under a rounded or triangular pediment. On the fine second-century gravestone illustrated on page 42 – that of a High Priestess of the Mother of the Gods, or Cybele, now in the Vatican Museum – the dignified half-length portrait of the dead woman is almost overshadowed by the immense scallop shell against which she stands in the act of pouring a libation. Occasionally, on the other hand, the shell is shown without the bust at all, as a substantive element of the monument. Later, under the Middle and Later Empire, when inhumation replaced cremation, the shell-medallion was retained on stone or marble sarcophagi, still as a background to the busts and sometimes supported by Cupids or Tritons. In the fourth century and later it was occasionally used also on Christian sarcophagi. There it might be associated with Biblical scenes, taken both from the

39

Marble sarcophagus from Sidamara, Asia Minor.

Old and the New Testaments; or the scalloped niches of the architectural tradition might be preferred as a framework for sacred monograms and the palm trees of paradise, as in the example illustrated overleaf. One gravestone, in the Villa Albani at Rome, bears within the shell the reclining figure of the dead woman with a child and a pet dog behind her; the whole composition recalling vividly the traditional representation of Venus and Cupid and thus illustrating the conscious or unconscious conservatism of the sculptor's repertoire.

In a less pictorial sense but still in a funerary context, the scallop is not infrequently used in the decoration of Roman lead coffins. An example in the Cinquantenaire Museum at Brussels, bearing eight-rayed stars, dolphins, and scallop shells framed by bead-and-reel mouldings, is said to have come from Syria; but the use of the shell as a coffin-ornament was especially characteristic of south-eastern England. From Kent, Essex, and above all the London district, something like twenty instances of late Roman lead coffins bearing the scallop pattern are recorded. One of them, now amongst those preserved in the British Museum, was found in London within an elaborately decorated stone sarcophagus; others had been encased in wood or stone, or buried without covering. On one of them, from South London, the scallops were associated with figures of the goddess Minerva.

Then again, there are many instances of the use of the scallop as an adjunct to domestic utensils of one kind or another. Flasks and other vessels of earthenware or glass sometimes assume the form of the scallop, such as the graceful example here illustrated (page 44) from the Rhineland, where much glass of a high quality was produced during the Middle and Later Empire. The shell occurs not infrequently as the hinged cover of the filling-hole of bronze lamps dating from the fourth or fifth century A.D., as seen in the plate on page 46. At a much earlier date, a silver ladle or wine-sampler in the form of a scallop was buried with the famous treasure of Boscoreale by the eruption that overwhelmed Pompeii, nearby. It has been observed that the model for this ladle was probably a scallop shell from the Indian Ocean; a suggestion which is historically reasonable in view of the active trade that subsisted between the Empire and India at this time. Other examples of scallops in bronze or silver have been found at Pompeii itself and may be seen in the museum at Naples. Some of them may have been used as pastry-moulds, others to hold poached eggs, or fish, or oil, or fruit. To some, small projections have been added to ensure steadiness on the table. In one way and another, the scallop motif must have been a familiar feature of the Roman dining-table. In more purely ornamental form, it was to be found also in the boudoir; for example, in the Archaeological Museum at Florence is an attractive bronze mirror-case from Perugia, with a carefully reproduced scallop as the central decoration.

These varied examples will suffice to illustrate the wide range of the scallop motif between the fourth century B.C. and the fifth or sixth century A.D. in lands which were at some time included within the Roman Empire. The problem remains to analyse these examples from the standpoint of function or intent. How far, in any particular instance, was a religious or symbolical purpose consciously present to artist or patron? How far did the scallop become a purely conventional and traditional ornament, of no more significance than the palmette or the ovolo? Was there a halfway stage between the two extremes, when the motif was

Tombstone of a High Priestess of the goddess Cybele: Roman, second century A.D.

regarded as 'correct' or even 'lucky' or prophylactic, without more serious import? Any historical account of a decorative unit so individual as the scallop must fall short without some discussion of the minds of its users in relation to it.

The earliest examples, as we have seen, relate to Aphrodite or Venus, in particular apparently to her birth. Here at once alternatives confront us. According to Homer, the goddess was the daughter of Zeus and Dione; a slightly later version, which dominates the literary tradition, has it that she was born from the sea-foam, fertilized by the heavenly Uranos. Certainly she was associated with the sea, was patroness of seafaring, and was, above all, 'Anadyomene', She who rose from the Sea. It has been held accordingly that the scallop shell associated with her in Hellenistic terra-cottas and vase-paintings is no more than a symbolical reminder that she was sea-born; the shell being technically an easier pictorial or sculptural device than the waves themselves. That may in fact be the right interpretation. But there is another possibility. Plautus, who wrote his comedies in the third century B.C., remarks of the goddess, 'They say that thou wast born from a shell'; and it is likely enough that, like much else, he was borrowing this version from a Greek predecessor. His is, however, the only surviving literary authority for it. A much later writer (Sextus Pompcius

Byzantine sarcophagus. Sixth century A.D.

Roman perfume flask of glass.

Phoenician coin, obverse and reverse, found at Saguntum, Spain. Second–first century B.C.

Festus, of the second century A.D.) affirms indeed that the Cytherean Venus derived her name from the town of Cythera, 'to which she is said first to have been carried by a shell, after being conceived in the sea'; but that is another matter, one on which Botticelli and Festus are in agreement. At least Plautus has behind him the solid backing of a whole series of Greek terra-cottas, which can scarcely imply anything other than the actual natal emergence of Aphrodite from betwixt the opening valves of the shell.

In any case, the general intent of these early representations is clear enough: to recall the nativity of the goddess of creative nature, concerned alike with sea and land. The initial emphasis on the sea may have owed something to the early maritime wanderings of the Aphrodite cult. Behind her classical embodiment lies the widespread worship of an Asiatic goddess of fertility, dating back perhaps to pre-neolithic times. Aphrodite herself in her Syrian embodiment, according to one obscure legend, was hatched out of an egg recovered by fishermen from the Euphrates. More immediately, she seems to have reached the Greek world from Phoenicia, whence she came with traders and colonists to the Greek islands. Herodotus in the fifth century B.C. recorded that the temple of the Heavenly Aphrodite at Ascalon in Palestine was said to be 'the oldest of all the temples of the goddess, for the temple in Cyprus was founded from it, as the Cyprians themselves say: and the temple on Cythera was founded by Phoenicians from this same land of Syria'. The recurrent association of the goddess with the scallop, whatever the local details of her legend, was a lasting reminder of her affinity with the sea and of her special concern for an element with which her travels at least had made her familiar. Whether as parent or as vehicle, the shell was widely regarded as

45

Two-branched bronze lamp: Roman.

an appropriate offering at her shrines, and tended even to assume a certain sanctity of its own as an emblem of the sea on the one hand and of fertility on the other. It may have been as a badge of the sea-goddess that the scallop occurs on the coins of several coastal towns: of Tarentum in southern Italy, for example, or of Saguntum in Spain (illustrated on page 45), where Carthaginian or Phoenician influence may have been at work. It should be added that the vogue of the scallop in the Aphrodite cult was shared with the murex, which supplied the famous Tyrian purple dye and was itself a stimulus to Phoenician colonization.

But whether and in what degree the Greeks of the fourth or third century B.C. took their pretty terra-cotta Aphrodites seriously is less certain. By that time the Hellenic instinct for beauty was in the ascendant, and the established gods and goddesses served the needs of art at least as devotedly as the artists served the needs of religion. Aphrodite in particular furnished the sculptor and the painter with abundant excuse for rendering the beauties of young womanhood, with only the sketchiest subservience to her divinity. In the Hellenistic household a sort of 'St Sulpice' craftsmanship continued to fulfil religious propriety but there too can have done little to satisfy any very genuine religious aspiration. Behind the conventional myths and cults there was now a whole range of new philosophies on the one hand and of mystical and secret rituals on the other, both more apt to the minds of an adult folk. Our terra-cotta poppets with their scallop shells sustained the conventions of the traditional religion, but it would be hard to say how far, if at all, this function matched their secular charm in the minds of their possessors.

Between this mythological usage of the scallop and its adoption as an architectural form in the head of a niche there is no manifest link, although rare instances, exemplified above, of the representation of Aphrodite in the scalloped head of a niche might suggest a possible transition. The shell-niche may indeed have been used more widely than we know to house figures of Aphrodite or of nymphs related to her cult in public and garden architecture. A good deal of ingenuity has in fact been expended upon attempts to find in this and other fashions a significant connexion between the religious and the architectural associations of the shell, but without any very solid result. The scallop is of a form peculiarly suited to the half-dome of the niche, and therein may be assumed to lie the main cause of its popularity amongst architects, when once the fashion had been established, as it may be supposed to have been, by some outstanding example no longer identifiable. On slender evidence, though not without probability, the original home of the half-domed niche or doorway has been sought in the Near or Middle East, where brick building rather than the timbered or trabeate construction of the Mediterranean lands was native and the half-domed niche would be technically a more natural development. The interpenetration of Hellenistic and Roman society by religious ideas from Asia Minor and Syria was certainly accompanied by the introduction of other ideas of a more material kind from the same sources – following vaguely indeed, at long range, the initial wanderings of Aphrodite or Venus herself. It may be guessed, then, that the scallop device, as a particular and pleasing variety of the half-dome, itself arrived with these Near Eastern influences somewhere in the third century B.C.; but time and place are alike unwitnessed. That the earliest dated example, as we have seen, occurs in Syria in the first century B.C. is no adequate proof that the type was evolved there, though it is consistent with the general supposition. At any rate, by the first century A.D. it was in almost universal use as part of the *lingua franca* of Roman architecture.

Was there any surviving vestige of a religious or semi-religious concept behind this vogue for the scallop in Graeco-Roman design? In particular, was there any meaning in the representation of the scallop on Roman gravestones and coffins? Occasionally, as on the Vatican gravestone of the High Priestess of Cybele mentioned above, the scallop is so emphatically rendered as to suggest that it possessed a specific significance. In other instances, the possibility of some remote nexus with the sea-born Aphrodite is rendered not unlikely when the shell-medallion on the sarcophagus is supported by sea-monsters, Tritons, in the hallowed tradition. The scallop shells which, as we have seen, occur not infrequently on Roman lead coffins, particularly in the London region, might be regarded as a mere ornament; but if the alleged discovery of five actual scallops within a Roman lead coffin at Angers on the Loire in 1848 is correct, we are at once compelled to seek some more recondite meaning.

Shells of one kind or another had indeed, as already remarked, a long and varied significance of a religious or symbolical sort in their own right. As late as the Middle Ages, for example, snails emerging from their shells were used to symbolize the resurrection; and the association of the scallop with the birth of Aphrodite or with her emergence from the sea, may, by an easy transition, have embodied the thought of the journey into the unknown or of resurrection after death. Once again, it is not necessary to assume that every undertaker who impressed the image of a scallop upon his lead coffins was consciously adding to the efficacy of his wares, or that his customers were filled thereby with other-worldly hope. It is enough to suppose that, from an initial credence, a convention had come into being that it was the right thing to include this element in the funerary craftsman's repertoire. In this sense there may, after all, have been a thin connecting thread between the Scallop of the Rising Goddess with which our story began and the Scallop of the Rising Soul with which it has ended.

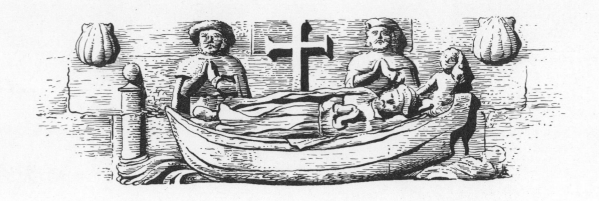

THE BADGE

OF ST JAMES

Christopher Hohler

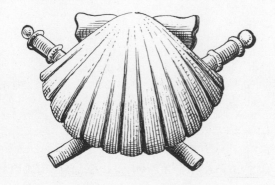

The Pilgrim Madonna: Pontevedra, Spain.

THE most charming of the monuments which adorn the town of Pontevedra in the far north-west of Spain is a little church built in 1778. A splendid curving baroque façade flanked by elegant towers covers a narrow entrance porch. This leads into a circular nave with a dome enriched with carved ribs and carrying a central lantern. The plan of the building was, we know, intended to represent a scallop shell; though the architect by curving his façade sacrificed zoology to art. The chancel has square sacristies on either side, thus ingeniously introducing the cross as well as the scallop into the design; and the purpose of the whole curious conceit is revealed by the image over the main altar. This is illustrated on the opposite page.

Clothed in silk, she appears to be a lady of the late eighteenth century dressed to go riding. The brim of her big white hat is turned up in front and in the middle is a large gold scallop. This is Our Lady *la Peregrina*, the blessed Virgin as a Pilgrim, a devotion so far as I know peculiar to Pontevedra, whose origins are far from clear.

In the middle of the façade, over the door outside, *la Peregrina* is represented again, in stone, between two male figures of more familiar aspect. Both have the same big hats and are liberally bedecked with scallop shells. They are St James the Greater and St Roch, also dressed as pilgrims. The scallop makes St James a pilgrim to his own tomb, and St Roch a pilgrim of St James though he actually went to Rome; but indisputably it is the transference of this symbol to Our Lady which is the most unexpected latest-ripened fruit of the belief that the apostle James was buried in Spain at Compostela. This belief, together with the stories of his personal intervention to bring victory to Christian armies fighting the Infidel is the reason for his being the patron saint of Spain, and there are countless Spanish works of art showing him on his charger, sword in hand, trampling the defeated enemy.

The legend of St James as told in the Middle Ages was decked out with much fabulous detail. In its final form it related how soon after the Ascension he undertook the evangelization of Spain. He had little success and returned with a few disciples to Jerusalem. Here he converted the pupil of a magician called Hermogenes. Hermogenes in dudgeon ordered his devils to fetch St James before him; but this resulted in the devils being tortured by angels and then sent back by St James to bind and bring Hermogenes. The magician on arrival hastily recognized his errors and was released; and since, as he pointed out, the devils after

St James the Greater and St John: Camara Santa, Oviedo, Spain. 1170–80.

their painful experience were thirsting for revenge, the saint gave him his staff which would be a sure protection. Shortly after this (as the Acts of the Apostles record) he was beheaded by Herod Agrippa. His disciples rescued his remains and carried them down to the sea, where they found a miraculous boat in which they embarked the body. When they were aboard a superhuman power brought them back to the scene of their master's preaching, to the port of Iria, now Padron, which belonged to a rich pagan lady called Lupa. They went to her and asked for a burying place for the saint. She referred them to the 'king' who threw them into prison. When they were miraculously released, he set after them with an army, only to meet his doom with all his men through the collapse of a bridge.

The disciples then returned to Lupa, who sent them to fetch some oxen which were really wild bulls. Killing a dragon on the way, they tamed the bulls with the sign of the cross, harnessed them to a cart on which they placed St James's body, and again presented themselves before Lupa. These wonders were enough to convert her, she handed over her palace, and there St James was buried, and with him in the fulness of time the two disciples who remained to watch over his grave, Athanasius on his right hand and Theodore on his left. What ultimate element of truth there may be in this it is hardly possible to say. What is certain is that the story of St James's preaching was known to St Aldhelm of Malmesbury who died in 709 and that the news that his body had been discovered in Galicia had reached Lyon in France by about 850.

Galicia, the Spanish province which looks on the map like a continuation northwards of Portugal, was apparently overrun like the rest of Spain by the Arab invaders between 712 and 717; but it then secured effective independence under the native rulers of the Kingdom of the Asturias. At this time Iria was the seat of a bishop, whose see was subject to the archbishop of Braga, a city now in Portugal. According to an eleventh-century document the burial place of St James, which had been forgotten, was revealed in a vision to a hermit called Pelayo who told Theodemir, bishop of Iria. Theodemir found the bodies of the apostle and his two disciples, and king Alfonso II of the Asturias (791–842) built a church on the site, which rapidly displaced that of Iria as the cathedral of the diocese. This story is inherently probable, the dates fit and it has recently received as clear confirmation as could be hoped from the discovery, within what are evidently the foundations of Alfonso II's church, of the gravestone of Bishop Theodemir. The name of the place, Saint James (Santiago) of Compostela, has furthermore been said to come from *Campus Stellae*, the Field of the Star, and connected with the mysterious lights which formed the core of Pelayo's vision; but this is less acceptable, as there are villages of the same name in Portugal, and it is probably a much older denomination than Pelayo's time, with quite a different etymology.

The shrine long enjoyed only a local fame. When in 997 the town of Santiago was sacked by the great Arab warrior Almanzor, one might have expected a wave of horror and indignation to sweep Christendom, although the actual tomb was apparently spared. In fact, however, the French chroniclers, and even the annalist working apparently at Coimbra in present-day Portugal, who wrote soonest after the event do not even allude to it, though they mention Almanzor; and it is evident that there was still no widespread veneration felt for the apostle's grave in the early eleventh century. St James nevertheless did have important devotees in southern France. There is accidental record of devotion by a bishop of le Puy as early as 950, and William Taillefer, Duke of Aquitaine, who died in 1028, paid numerous visits. Moreover, until the legends of St Mary Magdalen began to circulate in the later eleventh century, St James was the only prominent New Testament figure apart from SS. Peter and Paul whose grave was agreed to be in Europe. When, therefore, in the course of this same eleventh century the general tightening up of ecclesiastical discipline led to an increase in pilgrimage as such, Santiago was in a position of advantage which it has retained. After Jerusalem and Rome it is still the third pilgrimage of Christendom, and its badge is the scallop shell.

The concept of pilgrimage is a complicated one. Originally there were two strands: the devout visit to the lands of the Bible and the veneration of the graves of the martyrs. For the medieval development, however, a third strand was more important, namely the Irish idea of penance. This is a fascinating subject on which information is not perhaps very readily available; but it is quite impossible in the present context to give more then a condensed (and therefore inevitably slightly distorted) review of the facts. Briefly the Irish, between the sixth and eighth centuries, introduced Europe to a system of fixed penances, normally long periods of fasting, graduated according to the seriousness of sins privately confessed. This system in the long run proved unsatisfactory both spiritually and practically. It was not, however, formally disavowed, but rendered inoperative by various forms of commutation of which, from the eleventh century, the papal indulgence was the most important. By the end of the thirteenth century the effect of this had been to reduce the severity of the kind of penance a confessor would actually impose to a point where the periods of time specified in Bulls of Indulgence lost their original significance. But penitential exercises to which indulgences were attached continued to be popular, indeed appear to have gained steadily in popularity.

Pilgrimage, normally to Rome, entered this system in the ninth century as a controlled form of the Irish penance of exile, imposed for really serious offences. But it was generalized, since it proved to be a penance which the laity were prepared to undertake; and though its importance as an imposed penance had waned by about 1200, this was offset by the indulgences obtainable by visiting specified sanctuaries. Where these indulgences were wanting or insufficient, spurious grants by early Popes were liable to be fabricated. Pilgrimage was furthermore taken into the penal system of civil courts, notably in the Low Countries; and it was freely imposed on re-converted heretics in the early thirteenth century by the newly founded Inquisition.

As a penitent the pilgrim was presumed to be travelling on foot. From the early ninth century the scrip or bag and the staff which he therefore took with him were blessed before he set out. He was provided with a letter of recommendation and was expected to bring home a certificate that he had actually reached his destination. Penitential pilgrimage at all times tended to be undertaken by the less well-to-do since the rich could often commute it for almsgiving.

The rates of redemption, in Civil Courts at least, can be gauged from the fascinating conversion tables of the end of the Middle Ages which survive in the archives of several Flemish

Detail of a relief of the 'Last Judgement', including two pilgrims: Autun Cathedral, France. 1130–40.

towns. That of Termonde, for example, envisages redemptions ranging from 6*s* for the visit to St Wandrille by Coolscamp to £60 for that to São Thomé in Portuguese India, presumably reached via the Cape. Rome and Santiago were both assessed at £12.

Penitents undoubtedly formed the great bulk of eleventh and twelfth century pilgrims to Santiago, but the later indulgence seekers were scarcely less numerous. No fewer than 2,310 set sail for Spain from English ports alone in 1434, which was a Holy Year. Besides these, there were on the one hand always a certain number of more or less devout tourists and persons in search of miraculous cures; and on the other a good many ordinary tramps, and merchants hoping to avoid tolls under colour of religion. Among the last an exceptionally curious case was presented by a gentleman, calling himself Count of Lesser Egypt and travelling with a large retinue, whose bona fides was challenged at Jaca in 1435. He was in fact certainly a gypsy leading his tribe into Spain, and one of the earliest of whom there is clear record.

Exactly how Santiago in the eleventh century diverted so large a proportion of the potential pilgrims from Rome is a matter for speculation. Rome disliked the pretensions of Santiago, and its bishop was excommunicated in 1049 for using the words 'apostolic see' in his title. Cluniac propaganda has been held responsible, but this theory breaks down on the silence of all sources connected with the abbey of Cluny itself. Cluny and Rome were, however, certainly interested in war against the Infidel; and the pilgrimage, already popular in southern and western France, would seem to have benefited accidentally from the recruiting of northern French soldiery for various campaigns in Spain beginning in 1063. There is no evidence that the pilgrimage was organized in the modern sense. There was no equivalent of the char-a-banc party with a priest in charge. Accommodation along the main roads was provided, in accordance with the Rule, by monasteries which happened to exist, and by hospitals, founded by special benefactions and staffed by canons, which were hardly ever connected with monasteries, Cluniac or other, and appear to have come into being sporadically to meet an obvious need. But plenty of pilgrims at all times made use of ordinary inns.

The idea that the pilgrimage was organized is an over-hasty deduction from one eccentric and problematic book, the *Liber Sancti Jacobi*, of which the master copy is still at Santiago. Its author falsely used the name of Pope Calixtus II (1119–1124) and at the end he placed a species of Baedeker, improperly called the Pilgrim's Guide. This Guide, written about 1130, entertaining like other parts of the book and at times indecent, would have been most unsuitable, and in many ways curiously unpractical, for the pious penitent. It was clearly composed for the general edification of the clergy by a man anxious to popularize the pilgrimage but whose point of view was that of a traveller on horseback. The book as a whole is only about three parts serious. It has been described as a colossal fraud, but it could not possibly have deceived any reasonably sophisticated contemporary. It is indeed obvious that its writer (a Poitevin and apparently the ex-chaplain of a Latin Patriarch of Jerusalem) and its recipient (most probably Don Pedro Elias, Dean of Santiago from 1122 and Archbishop from 1143) must have known one another very well indeed. It was, however, the fruit of considerable industry and an abstract, omitting embarrassing elements such as the Guide, was in fact prepared for the use of visitors. Of this abstract a great many copies survive, including a fine twelfth-century one in the Royal Library at The Hague, whereas copies of the whole book are rare and mostly late. Like all other propaganda for Santiago, these books emanate from Santiago itself; but the name and aid of Cluny which had extensive connexions in Spain was invoked by Santiago, in particular by Bishop Diego Gelmirez (1100–1140), the most energetic of all occupants of the see, who succeeded in getting it raised to an archbishopric.

The first literary evidence for the scallop being the badge of the pilgrimage to Santiago is in the *Liber Sancti Jacobi*. The Guide states that shells to be attached to pilgrims' cloaks were on sale (about 1130) in the booths around the paved court north of the cathedral. Elsewhere in the book there is an account of how in 1106 a knight of Apulia was cured of the goitre by the touch of a shell brought home by a pilgrim; and a mystical explanation of the badge, the two valves of the shell symbolizing the Two Great Commandments and the markings fingers with which we perform good works, appears in the book also in a sermon. The earliest representation of a pilgrim wearing the shell (attached to his scrip) is on the west doorway of Autun Cathedral in Burgundy which also dates from about 1130 to 1140. Moreover the question addressed to Christ by the disciples on the road to Emmaus 'Art thou only a stranger in Jerusalem . . .' can be rendered, from the Latin, 'Art thou only a pilgrim . . .' and the pseudo-Calixtus duly develops the theme of Christ the first Pilgrim in one of his sermons. Accordingly in the cloisters of Santo Domingo de Silos in Spain and Arles in Provence there are sculptures showing Christ and the two disciples dressed as pilgrims, the scallop shell being much in evidence. The statues at Arles cannot be much earlier than 1160. The carving at Silos, if it depends on the pseudo-Calixtus, can hardly be earlier than 1130 which, in my

'Christ with the two disciples on the road to Emmaus': Santo DomIngo, Silos, Spain.

St James and St Peter: Leon Cathedral, Spain. Late thirteenth century.

view, is about right; but it is highly controversial and dates as early as 1070 have been proposed. It is clear, in any case, that the pseudo-Calixtus did not know (or was not prepared to disclose) the origin of the badge. His symbolic explanations are of the kind invented to justify some existing custom, and the story of a horseman, saved from drowning by St James, who found on emerging from the waves that both he and his horse were covered with scallops, cannot be traced further back than the sixteenth, or possibly the fifteenth century.

The last story is something of a puzzle as it exists in a great many forms. In a version printed in 1615 the horseman is an ancestor of the important Galician family of Pimentel, who swims his horse across an arm of the sea while on pilgrimage. There is no suggestion that he is in danger of drowning: the miracle consists solely in his becoming covered with scallops (apparently already the pilgrims' badge) and causes him to introduce a quartering of *vert five escallops argent* into his coat of arms. This may well be the original form: but, as printed in 1551, it was already used to account for the badge as well as the coat of arms. In this earlier version the horseman swims after the boat in which the disciples are bringing back St James' body. Versions datable to 1527 and, less reliably, 1441 have been mentioned, but no details are available. The genesis of this legend, therefore, requires further investigation.

But, whatever its original form, the legend does however draw attention to a particularly odd aspect of the scallop badge, namely that Santiago is not on the sea. One's thoughts turn to Padron, though the pseudo-Calixtus does not suggest that anyone usually visited it, and Padron itself is some distance up a navigable stream. This flows into a fairly long sea-loch; but even on the beaches of the loch scallop shells were anything but common when I was there. Undamaged ones have a market value as souvenirs which may go some way to explain this, and the place has been over-fished. But the fact remains that, by and large, scallops do have to be fished, fished from boats, and any available at Santiago in the early twelfth century would have had to be brought some sixteen miles over the hills on carts or donkeys. They were presumably therefore brought there in the first place for food, as they are now; and one can well imagine some enterprising hawker calling out that they came from the sea like St James. The choice of the shell in preference to any other emblem must in any case have been something of an accident for, since it cannot be traced before the twelfth century, it can hardly derive from a hypothetical pagan cult. Any decision to have a formal badge at all is indeed most improbable before the twelfth century; and the evidence points to this decision having been taken in Diego Gelmirez's time in imitation of Jerusalem. The pilgrim bound for Jerusalem wore a cross blessed by the Church, such as is shown on the scrip of a second figure on the Autun doorway; and he returned with a palm, with which the pseudo-Calixtus specifically contrasts St James's shell. The Roman pilgrim on the other hand had at this time no distinctive emblem, and badges for other European shrines do not seem to be attested before the fourteenth century, though no doubt they existed by the thirteenth. The tokens of the Jerusalem pilgrimage themselves are unlikely to have been standardized before the Latin capture of the city in 1099, the service for blessing the crosses cannot be traced earlier, and there

The reputed 'Pilgrims' Way': Padron, Spain.

is every chance that the story of the Apulian miracle was circulated soon after the adoption of the badge in order to popularize it. If so this adoption took place between 1099 and 1106.

The circumstances under which the scallop badge was transferred to St James himself are also somewhat mysterious. There are statues of the apostle at Santiago, datable to about 1120 and about 1180, neither of which shows it; but the later of the two, that on the west porch of the cathedral, holds a short tau-headed staff. This is not a pilgrim's staff, it is normally the mark of an abbot; but here it probably has reference to the staff which St James is said to have given to Hermogenes, and which was (and is) exhibited at Santiago. By 1180, however, there were already at least two statues in Spain, one on the jamb of the west door of the abbey church of Santa Marta de Tera (about 1140–50?) and the other in the set of caryatid apostles in the Camara Santa at Oviedo (about 1170–80?), showing the saint dressed like any other apostle but with the genuine attributes of the pilgrim. These attributes, the two which were formally blessed, were the scrip (adorned on these statues with the scallop) and the long staff (though at Oviedo this ends in a cross and banner like that of the Risen Christ).

In this precise form the fashion for showing St James with the attributes of a pilgrim never spread further than Gascony. Bordeaux marks the limit, but there are other statues of this kind, of various and uncertain dates in the thirteenth century, at Bayonne, Mimizan, and probably (the statue is damaged) Dax. All these Gascon examples imply a knowledge of the great north French cathedral doorways, and the earliest, the second-rate statue at Mimizan,

The Way to Compostela

According to the 12ᵀᴴ century "Guide"

The Pilgrim routes to Santiago de Compostela. Roman roads are represented by unbroken lines. The dotted lines indicate possible deviations, as suggested by Jose Maria Lacarra to account for the places mentioned in the 'Guide'. The underlined place-names are referred to in the text.

has extra scallops on the strap of the scrip, a detail characteristic of the statues of St James at Reims and Amiens. But in whichever direction this particular detail was transmitted, the distribution of the group and the early date of the Spanish examples make it evident that the idea of distinguishing St James from other apostles simply by putting the scrip over his shoulder and the staff in his hand originated in Spain. One can only guess that the great public decided that the tau-staff of some predecessor of the Santiago statue had reference to the pilgrimage, and that Spanish sculptors accepted and developed this point of view.

It is commonly thought that the four 'routes of St James' across France described in the Pilgrim's Guide were intimately connected with the spread of the habit of representing St James in this way. The four routes, however, with minor detours (usually to famous sanctuaries) are the four roads leading to the Pyrenees set out in the Roman road-books called the Antonine Itinerary and the Peutinger Tables. They link up all the principal towns and a pilgrim coming from any distance would obviously sooner or later have found his way on to one of them. But pilgrims could start from and return to anywhere; and far from spreading along these roads from Spain, the Spanish way of representing St James seems to have been transplanted directly to north-east France and disseminated in freshly developed forms from there.

The evidence available to decide this point is practically limited to statues, among which there may have been important losses, not to mention examples unknown to me; and it would be dangerous to be too categorical. Certain facts seem clear, nevertheless. Among surviving

61

An Italian painting of St James: Simone Martini and assistants. Fourteenth century.

St James as embroidered on the 'Syon Cope': English. Late thirteenth century.

twelfth-century series of apostles in France, St James is not distinguished by any special emblem. The early thirteenth century groups, at Reims, Amiens, and Chartres, show him, however, with the scallop-decked scrip, but no staff, a book, and the sword of his martyrdom. The separation of scrip and staff in this way is anomalous, and the slightly later statue at the church of La Couture at Le Mans, belonging to the same group, shows him uncomfortably wielding a sword in one hand and a staff in the other. But this, in view of the relative dates, must be a modification of the Reims type. And as the combination of sword and scrip is peculiar to these north French statues it must be of local invention.

Another type represented on English embroideries from about 1280 and by a beautiful mid-fourteenth-century statue in the choir of Cologne Cathedral shows the saint either without any scrip or carrying it in the same hand as his staff. This again seems to have been unknown at the time in Spain and the context of the English and German examples demands a French model, probably in this case the statue in the set of apostles placed on corbels round the Sainte Chapelle in Paris about 1240–50. These statues have not all survived, most of those that have are without their original attributes, and the one sometimes called St James

Silver altar-piece by Gilio Pisano in the Cathedral of Pistoja, Italy. 1349.

the Greater holding something which might be a staff, is probably St James the Less with a fuller's bat. However, none of the existing figures ever had a scrip over his shoulder and the Cologne statue is one of a set placed on corbels in the same way.

The French origin of the Cologne type of St James is the more certain in view of the marked reluctance of both German and Italian artists to show an apostle in any sort of fancy dress. In German painting the apostle is constantly depicted without any allusion to the pilgrimage until well on in the fifteenth century, and in Italy such allusions are always the exception, even in legendary scenes connected with Spain. The fourteenth-century paintings by Altichiero at Padua, for instance, show the translation of the saint's body to Iria, his appearance in a vision to King Ramiro of the Asturias, and his subsequent intervention in the battle of Clavijo against the Moors, without any use of the scallop at all. There appears, too, to be no trace of the scallop as St James's emblem in Italian painting earlier than that on a polyptych by Deodato Orlandi at Pisa dated 1301, when it is merely a single shell attached to the apostle's cloak. In Germany the equivalent concession to Franco-Spanish fashions was to show the apostle carrying a scallop in his hand. This arrangement is found about 1250 on the Paradise door of Paderborn Cathedral, and a century later on the north transept of the cathedral at Cologne.

In the late thirteenth century an entirely new departure is marked by the representation of St James wearing a pilgrim's hat. The hat was not blessed by the Church and its introduction is a piece of deliberate realism. With or without the scallop it becomes from this point on the most obvious distinguishing mark of St James; and as its form is almost infinitely variable, it sets a whole series of very intricate questions for the enquiring mind. The statement that a pilgrim naturally wore a broad-brimmed hat as a protection against sun and rain is promptly traversed by the existence of a late thirteenth-century statue on one of the doorways of Leon Cathedral wearing a tall dunce's hat with a scallop halfway up. This would have given no serious protection against either; and it was not a mere whim of the sculptor as is proved by the similar hats of the Emmaus group in the cloister at Arles. Leon Cathedral alone, moreover, has sculptures with at least three more versions of the hat; one rather like a beret is worn by the pilgrims on a carving of about 1240; another, round in the crown and with a long pointed peak, is worn by the St James in a lunette over a tomb of about 1280; and a third, resembling some sort of sou'wester, is worn by the St James of about 1300 among the statues of the west front. The interaction over the years between what pilgrims from different countries actually wore and what, owing to the influence of famous works of art, not only artists but pilgrims themselves thought they ought to wear, obviously provides material for lengthy study. Fortunately we are here concerned with scallops, not millinery; and, whatever the form of the hat, one or more scallops are almost always to be seen on its front, in the fifteenth century and later often flanked by the further emblem of a pair of crossed pilgrim's staves.

One particular aspect of the matter of hats does, however, deserve further mention. The silver altar-piece of the cathedral of Pistoja has at its centre a seated figure of St James wearing a hat rather like a Boy Scout's. This statue, made by Gilio Pisano in 1349, is

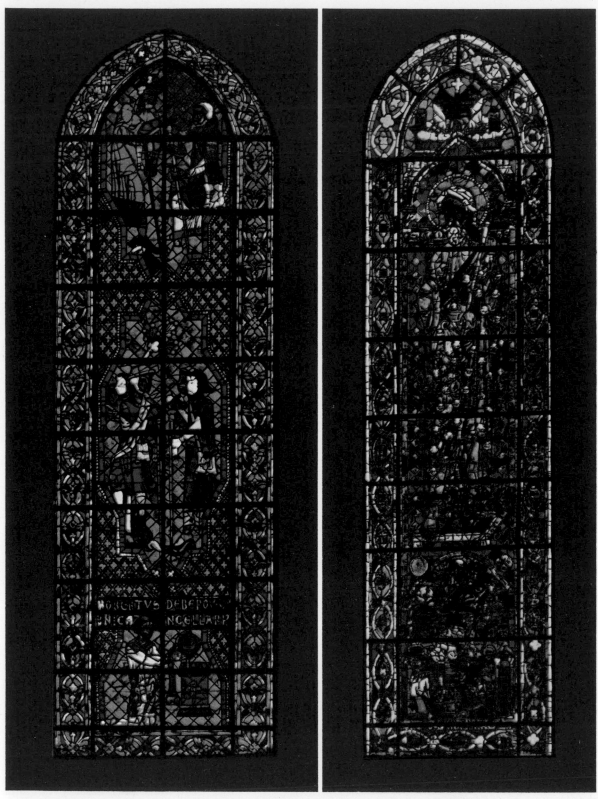

The stained glass of two windows in Chartres Cathedral: on the left is the Pilgrim window given by the Cathedral Chancellor, who died in 1216; on the right is the St James window given by the Bakers' Guild.

of a type which cannot possibly have originated in Italy and, in fact, the only closely similar seated image with a hat of the same general type is a stone figure in the museum at Beauvais. The wide separation of these two related and unusual statues makes it probable that both are copies of the most famous seated figure of St James then in existence. This was the one, now lost, carved by Robert de Lannoy between 1319 and 1327 which stood over the main altar in the chapel of the Confraternity of St James at Paris. It was itself presumably inspired by the seated statue of St James still enthroned above the high altar of Santiago Cathedral which is thought to be early thirteenth century; but this has no hat and it is likely that the present pilgrim's staff replaces an earlier tau-staff. This raises the general question of the part played by confraternities in the development and popularization of the conception of St James as a pilgrim.

The Paris Confraternity is the first of which there is unequivocal written record. It was founded about 1295 by and for returned pilgrims, though membership could be bought at the price of a pilgrimage. It maintained a hospice in Paris besides performing for its members the same religious and philanthropic services as any other medieval guild. Similar institutions were to be found at the end of the Middle Ages in most important towns in the Low Countries and probably also in Germany; but all those of which there is readily accessible record appear on the scene rather late and are under suspicion of being copies of the Confraternity at Paris. The 'Pilgrimage Roads' have nothing to do with the matter: if it is significant that there was such a Confraternity at Moissac which was on one of the Roads, it is also significant that it was not founded till 1523.

The only serious challenge to the seniority of Paris appears in fact to come from Chartres. The stained glass in the cathedral there includes five windows which together with the statue on the north door have a bearing on this question. The window in one of the aisles given by the corporation of furriers, which illustrates the saint's legend, is of interest as including a scene of Christ giving St James a staff. This scene for which there is no known literary basis once figured also in a clerestory window, liberally diapered with scallops and now destroyed, which was given by a king of Castille.

The single figure of the apostle in a clerestory window given by the merchant Geoffrey (who appears at the foot of it with his family, all dressed as pilgrims) is likewise set against a diaper of scallops, and that in the similar window given by the corporation of bakers has scallops all over his robe. The remaining window, also in the clerestory and given by a Cathedral Chancellor who died in 1216, shows nothing but scenes of pilgrimage which are so far unexplained. It is, however, difficult to account for this last window at all without accepting the suggestion that the Chancellor was head of a Confraternity of St James: and a Confraternity before 1216 would be startlingly early. This, in conjunction with the Castillian connexion and the number of St James windows in the cathedral, encourages the idea that St James with the emblems of pilgrimage was introduced into French art in the first place at Chartres itself.

It would be tedious to attempt to review the innumerable versions of the theme of St James as a pilgrim sculptured or drawn when, in the later Middle Ages, this type had become

St James with a kneeling donor: Kalkar, Germany. About 1500.

canonical. A particularly successful single figure, of the school of Jacomart of Valencia, formerly belonging to the church of Puebla de Vallbona may perhaps be given a special mention. It shows the saint in a combination of ecclesiastical and pilgrim dress which creates an effect of great splendour, contrasting oddly with the haunting melancholy of his face. Of more constant appeal, however, are those paintings illustrating the saint's legend, in which this fascinating incongruity of dress is joined to other interweavings of an imaginary dream-world with carefully observed details taken from life.

There is for instance a panel from Lerida, now in the Prado, which shows Theodore and Athanasius with the ox cart. The dead saint and his two disciples are all three wearing full pilgrim attire with scallops in their hats. Lupa dressed as a fine lady of the fifteenth century looks out of a window; and in the background appears the sea with the boat in which the party are still arriving. In the even more dream-like painting of the same subject by Nicolas Frances on the main altar-piece of Leon Cathedral the disciples, shown first taming the bull and then leading the cart on which lies the coffin covered by a gorgeous pall, are dressed for these activities as deacons with dalmatics of beautiful brocaded Italian silk. In the background are a shepherd and shepherdess with their sheep and a town with a Gothic cathedral which is

Palace with shells: Salamanca, Spain. Early sixteenth century.

probably meant for Santiago, for to the right of it is the wayside cross and heap of stones which once marked Montjoie, the hill from which the pilgrim first saw the city. Further to the right is a church, probably still meant for Santiago Cathedral, with one wall cut away to give a glimpse of a priest celebrating mass. To complete this massive rejection of the unities of time and place a pilgrim is shewn beside the wayside cross. Inside the church another pilgrim, with several scallop shells on his clothes, puts his offering into a money-box beside an altar; and above the altar stands a statue of the saint (whose body is still unburied) dressed as a pilgrim with the shells in his hat.

In the later Middle Ages it is normally paintings such as these and stained glass windows, rather than carvings, which provide the greatest pleasures. An exception must, however, be made in favour of a number of particularly splendid statues of St James in wood from German altar-pieces of the years around 1500. The theme of the ideal pilgrim made a particular appeal to their sculptors, and the figures in elaborately observed costume have a pathetic grandeur which has no obvious connexion with what is known or related about the apostle. It probably owes much to the legend of St Roch who provided the other chief opportunity to develop the pilgrim theme. St Roch of course is usually represented showing

69

the plague-spot on his leg; but there is little else to distinguish the two saints in German art except that St Roch ought not to be wearing the scallop, for in the Middle Ages the scallop does appear to have been the exclusive badge of the pilgrimage to Santiago.

There is indeed one known exception, the Mont Saint Michel off the coast of Normandy. An *ordonnance* of Charles VI of France, issued in 1393, refers to the booths of the sellers of shells there, the escallop is prominent in the arms of the abbey, attested from the late fourteenth century, and the commonest type of lead badge bought by pilgrims to the Mount in the fifteenth century shows the archangel in conjunction with one or more shells. Zoologically the shells actually found in the bay of Mont St Michel are of a species different from the St James's shell and have asymmetrical ears, but this feature is overlooked in artistic representations. Some marine symbol was clearly suitable for a pilgrimage to an island; but the shells of St Michael do not seem to have received any kind of official recognition at all early, and there can be little doubt that when it came it was in imitation of St James.

That St Michael in this way should purloin the emblem of St James was of course no small tribute to the extraordinarily effective quality of the symbol which the promoters of the Santiago pilgrimage had been inspired to adopt. It is difficult to believe that the magnate of Salamanca who diapered the whole front of his palace with carved scallops in the early sixteenth century was influenced solely by motives of piety. Certainly his family considered they owed much to the intervention of St James. But would he have expressed his gratitude in quite the same way, one wonders, if St James's emblem had been a tooth in a pair of pincers like St Apollonia, or a boot like Sir John Shorne? Conversely, might not Scotland, which after all claimed that the bones of another apostle lay at St Andrews, have attracted more pilgrims to its national shrine if the saltire had had the same subtlety of design as the scallop? It is idle perhaps to ask, in the sense that no final answer can be forthcoming. One can only say that as the scallop had no meaning apart from the pilgrimage, every statue, every painting, every stained-glass window showing St James with a scallop was another invitation to visit his grave. No other saint had a specific badge of pilgrimage which became his normal emblem; and apart from Jerusalem and Rome (where attraction was of a different order), no other pilgrimage drew such multitudes and has continued to draw them through the centuries.

THE CRADLE

OF VENUS

James Laver

'Venus Anadyomene': Titian, c.1520.

THE Renaissance was a Liberation of Symbols. Before, almost every element in Nature had been, as it were, pressed into the service of the Church. The scallop shell – to take the object which here interests us most – had been the symbol of St James, and the forms it took have just been considered by Christopher Hohler in the preceding chapter. As he has said, pilgrims to the shrine at Compostela wore it in their hats. It was a mark of devotion, a sign that the pilgrim had really travelled. But with the Renaissance this symbol, like everything else, became secularized. What had been a religious emblem became a decorative motif, to be used, without any special significance, as pleased the wish and the whim of the artist.

When we were young most of us thought that we knew what the Renaissance was and where it happened. It was equated with the Fall of Constantinople in 1453. Greek scholars, such was the story, took refuge in the West, and from that date onwards a revival of interest in the art and ideas of Ancient Greece and Rome can be noted all over Europe. Scholarship has an unhappy knack of blurring these clear-cut distinctions, these exact dates. It now seems that the Renaissance started much earlier, especially in Italy. Petrarch is sometimes hailed as the first modern man, but he was dead by 1374. Cimabue and even Giotto were not quite medieval figures in spite of the piety and traditionalism of their subject-matter. Some new wind was filling their sails, some new influence guided their pencils, some new notions stimulated their minds. The Renaissance has been compared with springtime, a spring bringing light and colour into human life again after the long night. Suddenly this world became something more than the dark antechamber of a hoped-for heaven; somehow the dry roots put forth new blossoms, and the individual was born anew.

It is difficult for us, in the modern world, to understand the state of mind of the men who were in the forefront of the new movement. For with us, the reverse process is taking place. We are coming to the end of a period of individualism. A new merging of man in the mass is taking place before our eyes. Perhaps that is why we have the sensation of an approaching frost when all individual activity will be subject to increasing controls and to the weight of an accepted ideology which leaves no room for private opinion. The feeling of the men who lived in the Renaissance period – however we may extend or narrow its limits – was one of immense release. Like the Europeans who first reached the Americas, they knew

Marble wash basin, ascribed to Rossellino: Fiesole, Italy. Late fifteenth century.

'The Birth of Venus': Botticelli, 1478.

they were entering a new world, a world of untried and boundless possibilities. It would have been strange indeed if this new attitude had not been reflected in their art.

The transition from art as religion to art as *décor* is typical of the whole Renaissance Movement. Even the actual personages of sacred story were not exempt, for if a Madonna by Cimabue is purely hieratic, and one by Fra Angelico purely religious in intention, a Madonna by Titian is simply a portrait of the artist's mistress. Rubens, a century later, went a stage further. We even find the name of the sitter: 'So-and-so as St Catherine', as a theatre programme might say 'So-and-so as Hamlet'. The actor, or actress, is frankly playing a part.

If the artists of the Renaissance were cutting loose from their Christian moorings, it was because they had, in effect, adopted a new set of values. One might almost call it a new religion: the Religion of Humanism. No longer was the reward of virtue to be postponed until the next world. Indeed, the word itself changed its meaning, and *virtu* meant the combination of qualities which ensured a man the immortality of Fame. The old Roman goddess Fortuna came into her own again and with her all the other deities of the pagan pantheon. Once more there were statues made of Bacchus and Venus, especially of Venus. She was the favourite of all, if only as an excuse for the newly-discovered interest in the nude human body. Painters and sculptors vied with one another to give her bodily form.

Perhaps the most famous of all such representations is Botticelli's *Birth of Venus*, now in the Uffizi at Florence. How narrowly she escaped! Only the happy chance that she was out of Florence when the fanatical Savonarola organized his 'bonfire of vanities' saved her from being quite literally burned at the stake. We might adopt her as the patron-goddess of our present study, for is she not wafted landward, poised upon a shell, the very shell with which we are now concerned? Other artists painted her too and even if Titian in his famous *Venus Anadyomene* does not actually show her as borne landward on a shell, at least he includes the shell in a corner of his picture.

It is very difficult, as we have said, to give an exact date for the beginning of the change. The more closely scholars study the Renaissance the earlier its first burgeonings appear. Even Fra Angelico, whom we have just mentioned as the very type of the religious painter, was not exempt from Renaissance motifs, or even from the decorative use of the shell. In his painting of *St Lawrence giving alms* in the Vatican he shows the saint standing before a pure Renaissance doorway with a vista of classical columns behind. The church, if such it be, is closed with a rounded apse, and the top part of the apse is the shell itself. In his *St Lawrence before Decius* in the same series, Decius sits upon a throne in a kind of niche surmounted by the same shell. Fra Angelico's follower Domenico di Michelino used it for his enthroned Madonna in the Louvre, and even more clearly in his *Madonna and Angels* in San Marco, Florence. Domenico Veneziano does the same in his *Madonna and Saints* in the Uffizi. In the same gallery is another *Madonna and Saints* by Filippo Lippi in which there are three niches, the central one having a kind of coffered ceiling and the outer two, shells.

The use of the shell in this way became almost a convention. It can be studied at the end of the fifteenth century in the work of Piero di Lorenzo, in Botticelli's figures of the Popes in the Sistine Chapel and in his painting of the *Madonna and Saints* formerly in a church in Florence. In an *Annunciation* from a private collection (reproduced in Raimond van Marle's monumental work on the *Italian Schools of Painting*) he adopts the curious compromise of using the shell as a *dessus-de-porte*, with a coat of arms affixed to it in the middle. Another unusual use of the shell is to be seen in a painting by Luca Signorelli in the Uffizi, where the head of Christ is seen inside the shell.

All the sculptured figures in Botticelli's famous *Calumny* in the same Florentine gallery stand in niches arched with shells. Filippino Lippi uses the shell in the same way for his *Madonna and Angels* in the Corsini Gallery, Florence, and for his *Triumph of St Thomas Aquinas* in Santa Maria sopra Minerva, in Rome. We find it again in the work of Raffaelino del Garbo; and, in the *Madonna and Saints*, in the Brera Gallery, Milan – a painting which is supposed to have been the work of several hands, including Piero della Francesca and Luca Signorelli – behind the virgin there is a deep niche formed by a shell, inverted this time, and from the point of which hangs an egg on a string. The interesting thing about this niche is that it is supposed to have been based upon the porch of an actual church, that of Sant' Andrea at Mantua, designed by no less a person than Alberti.

There is a drawing by Benozzo Gozzoli in the British Museum showing St Severus standing in a niche which is a most curious blend of Gothic and Renaissance elements.

English gilt-silver beaker. 1599.

But over the head of the saint is – the shell. He uses it again for the top of the academic chair of *St Augustine teaching philosophy in Rome*, a painting to be seen in the church of Sant' Agostino at San Gimmignano. The shell is found again in the embroideries after designs by Pollaiuolo preserved in the Cathedral of Florence. It is also to be seen in a flattened form in the sculptured tomb of Pope Innocent VIII by the same artist in St Peter's. Verrocchio uses it in the altar-piece of the Cathedral at Pistoja; Domenico Ghirlandaio for his in the church at Porozzi, near Florence. His brother Benedetto did the same in his painting in San Lorenzo in the same city. In the painting by Florenzo di Lorenzo, now in the Gallery at Perugia, the shell-surmounted niche is actually architectural, with the paintings round it. This architectural use of the shell as part of the framework of paintings can be seen again (there are actually five shells) in the polyptych painted by Giovanni Boccati for the church of Sant' Eustachio Belforte and, strangely mingled with Gothic arches, in a triptych in San Zaccaria, Venice. If we find the shell-niche so frequently depicted in painting, it is because it was already a commonplace in architecture.

Nor is there anything surprising in this. Sir Mortimer Wheeler in his essay in the present volume traces its use in Ancient Rome; and what is the Renaissance but the re-discovery of a buried world? One has only to visit the church of San Pietro in Montorio, to find in the little courtyard beside it, erected over the alleged site of the crucifixion of St Peter, one of the most influential architectural structures in the world. This is Bramante's Tempietto.

With its circular wall, its dome and its balustrade it is plainly the elder brother of St Peter's and (if the phrase may be permitted) the grandfather of St Paul's. Around the dome, above the balustrade, are niches each topped with the scallop; and inside the four great niches are similar in form. In one of them, above the high altar, sits St Peter himself.

Bramante's part in the design of the great St Peter's was limited to some preliminary designs and he cannot be held responsible for the decorative details. Yet the shell motif which he used in the Tempietto is to be seen both inside and out. The large niches in the vast façade show two shells, one inside the other, while the smaller niches, higher up and crowned with the Papal tiara, are also adorned with shells. The scallop tops the Porta Santa, and is to be found inside round the interior of the dome and also over the great niches in the nave from which gesticulate the heroic figures of saints. Luigi Capponi's saints in the church of St John Lateran are equally scallop-niched, as are all the Andrea Sansovino *Virtues* in Santa Maria del Popolo. The figures in Santa Maria Maggiore show the same use. So does Andrea Bregno's *St Michael* in the church of Santa Maria in Aracoeli, at the top of its endless flight of steps. The list might be extended indefinitely.

The palace builders were equally prone to use the scallop as a decorative motif. The first-floor windows of the palace on the Via Borgho Novo, once inhabited by Raphael, were interspersed with shell-topped niches. The circular courtyard of the former Curia Innocentiana is lined with double niches, the shell in the upper compartment; while the opposite effect, with the shell surmounting the inferior niches, is to be found on the façade of the Farnesina. In the Palazzo Farnese the gallery painted by Annibale Caracci has a row of statues in niches with the same decoration.

But the scallop comes most completely into its own, as it were, when it breaks away from the architectural façade and sets up for itself as a fountain. And Rome is full of fountains. In the great 'Moses' fountain in the Piazzi delle Terme the shell is still architectural, as it is to a lesser extent in the Trevi Fountain where the niche above Neptune is diapered and has at its apex a shell. But in Bernini's Triton Fountain in the Piazza Barberini the shell stands free. In fact there are two deep scallops lying horizontal with the triton riding atop. In the fountain in the corner of the same piazza we find both deep and flat shell, in fact the whole creature, wide open with water spurting forth.

Bernini made lavish use of the scallop in works of the most varied description carried out in the early years of the seventeenth century. We find it not only in his fountains, but in his religious monuments (as for example in the Chigi Chapel in Santa Maria del Popolo, where the Angel lifts the Prophet Habbakuk by his hair, under a shell-niche), and even in his portraits, as in the church of San Michele all'Isola in Venice where the bust of Cardinal Giovanni Dolfin is backed with a shell. This was a reversion to the usage of Ancient Rome.

In architecture and sculpture therefore the use of the shell continued well into the seventeenth century, but in painting it had long ceased. A century earlier painting had become more naturalistic, and so less given to formal backgrounds and figures placed formally in niches. The painting of Northern Europe was always so – although a painter

Fontana delle Api, 'The Bee Fountain': Piazza Barberini, Rome. 1644.

like Justus of Ghent, who worked from 1460 to 1480 and whose allegorical figure of *Music* is in the National Gallery, London, may be quoted as an exception. But if the scallop in the mid-sixteenth century disappears from painting, it holds its own not only in architecture and sculpture, as we have already seen, but in the arts of the goldsmith.

The Renaissance had introduced a much greater degree of luxury in interior decoration and in the appurtenances of the table; and the skill of those who had formerly produced vessels for the altar was now diverted to more mundane matters. Standing cups, goblets, dishes of all kinds, wrought in precious metals and elaborately chased and gadrooned, were a necessary part of the splendour of kings and nobles. The shell is itself a vessel and sometimes actual shells were used, the gold-mounted nautilus being a favourite. The scallop shell was not rare enough to be precious and so was seldom used in its natural form. But it was imitated in precious metals or used as a decorative motif.

Holbein employs it thus with striking effect. He had used it before he came to England as part of the architectural detail of his religious paintings, notably in his *Mater Dolorosa* at Basle. He uses the shell in its traditional form in the so-called *Madonna of Darmstadt*. In 1537 he was commissioned by Henry VIII to decorate the Privy Chamber in the Old Palace of Whitehall. This was unfortunately destroyed in the fire of 1698, but a fragment of the original cartoon survives in the Devonshire Collection. In it we see Henry VIII against a background of pilasters decorated with arabesques between which is a niche with the inevitable shell. Holbein used it also in his designs for dagger sheaths, and for painted glass.

One swallow does not make a summer. Holbein was a foreign artist visiting this country; it was a long time before England felt the full impact of the Renaissance. That impact reached France much earlier, with the School of Fontainebleau patronized by François I. In spite of the disasters of his reign he was a lavish patron of the arts; and there is today a peculiar charm in some of the buildings which he caused to be erected. The Chateau at Blois is generally accepted as a masterpiece of his period and the part of the palace facing the great courtyard shows a façade which is particularly interesting from our point of view. Surmounting a gabled window is an elaborate sculptured niche in which stands a nude female figure. Above her head is the scallop shell. Lower down is a whole row of such shells imbedded in small circular niches. The style of his successor Henri II is very similar. Examples of the shell ornament are frequent, as they are in the later style of Henri IV. The latter monarch is himself shown in effigy in a niche under a shell canopy above the great doorway of the *cour d'honneur* of the Capitole at Toulouse.

England by this time – the early years of the seventeenth century – was beginning to catch up with Continental taste. Ever since the time of Henry VIII, Italian designers had been at work in England but they were generally few in number. It has been well said that they were in sufficient numbers to modify native ornament but not native forms. A typical early example is Layer Marney in Essex, where the form of the house is English, the motifs Italian. These include the shell, several examples of which surmount the brick octagonal towers of the gatehouse. Shells appear again at the top of the panelling of the screen (dated 1581) at Cuckfield Park; again on the hall screen (*c*.1620) at Bowringsleigh, Devonshire, and also in the great

'Child blowing bubble': Pierre Mignard, c.1660.

French carpet made in La Savonnerie, France. 1660–1690.

hall at Hatfield. Chilham Castle has a shell at the top of each pilaster of the porch, and it forms part of the decoration of the great door of the hall at Ford House, near Newton Abbott, built by Sir Richard Reynell in the reign of James I.

In France the *Style Henri Quatre* merges imperceptibly into that of Louis XIII. But with Louis XIV, something else emerges: definitely a *Style Roi Soleil*, which was to exercise an enormous influence all over Europe. We find carved shells, each with a classical head in the middle, on the great doors of the Sorbonne; a positive fantasia of shells adorned the flattened arches of the windows of a house in the Rue du Cherche-Midi, in Paris. The splendid Fontaine de l'Abbaye in the Rue Childerbert in the same city showed a similar use of the shell motif, mingled with dolphins.

Examples could be multiplied; but it is perhaps in interior decoration that the *Style Louis Quatorze* is seen at its most characteristic. The dominating influence was that of Jean Bérain, who imposed a unity of style not only on panelling, ceiling decoration, and furniture, but also on stage-design and costume. His decorative panels show shells, often inscribed with the royal monogram. In one particularly fine example Neptune rides on a scallop shell drawn by two sea-horses. His fire-places are surmounted by shells, and his tapestry designs make

82

Wall cistern and basin: Delft pottery, Holland. Mid-eighteenth century.

frequent play with similar forms. Bérain's boulle-decorated side-tables almost always have a shell as their most important element.

In England in the early eighteenth century, Vanbrugh frequently employed the shell motif. A huge shell surmounts the chimney-piece in the great Saloon of Kimbolton Castle, one of his masterpieces. Shells are also to be seen in the even grander Saloon at Blenheim, surmounting the arched doorways. A most interesting use of shell ornament is to be found in the *trompe-l'œil* niche over the fireplace in the so-called Sabine Room at Chatsworth. This is by another hand, but contemporary. There are shell-niches in the loggia of Cranborne Manor, Dorset, also in the West Colonnade of Drayton House, Northamptonshire.

The stucco decorative work by Bagutti at Mereworth Castle, Kent, is of considerable interest. In the 'hanging gallery', beneath the dome, the doors are surmounted by enormous shells each containing a classical bust. The house was completed in 1723. The corners above the cornice in the drawing room show an original and striking use of the shell motif; and a similar use of it in the ceiling corners is to be seen at Moor Park, Hertfordshire. Armchairs in the William Kent style are likely to show shells in various parts, and so are the side-tables so typical of this designer's work. There is a very interesting example of this use at Houghton: a side-table supported by an almost life-size putto emerging from a shell. In the same great house the bed of state is backed by an enormous scallop. The shell was much used in wood-panelling as the top of a niche or cupboard-recess. There are interesting examples in the small dining room at Oulton Park, Cheshire, and at Rainham Hall, Essex.

The shell motifs in the stucco-work on the ceiling of the Library at Kirtlington Park, Oxfordshire, show traces of the rococo influence which in general did not obtain much scope in England. In France, of course, it was, for more than a generation, the dominant style. It was full of shells, indeed in one of its aspects it is known as *rocaille*, but the shells are treated with a freedom of fancy which leaves very little trace of their original form. They might be described as *exploding* shells; in fact the whole of the rococo is a kind of explosion disintegrating the formal modes of the previous century.

There was a frivolity about the rococo period in France which is not without its charm. 'Do not let us take things too seriously' it seemed to say, a sentiment which since the world began has never been incompatible with a certain melancholy. If we wanted a symbol of this we could not do better than contemplate some of the paintings of Antoine Watteau, that gallicized Fleming who created a whole new world of the imagination. His famous *Embarquement pour Cythère* is singularly appropriate to our present study; for the characters who move in the enchanted light of this beautiful canvas are actually pilgrims. They are even clothed in the pilgrims' habit – in an elegant and abbreviated form – and they wear by a final irony (one would be tempted to call it a blasphemy if the mood of the painting were less tender and delicate) the pilgrims' shell – the shell of Santiago.

The shell motifs in the panelling of the music *salon* in the Arsenal Library in Paris are of restrained and almost classical form; so are those in the *petit salon* of Versailles. But in the Archbishop's Palace at Bordeaux there is a curved chimney-piece which is a positive firework display of 'exploding shells'. It was, however, in Germany that the rococo style reached its

'Embarquement pour Cythère' (detail): Antoine Watteau, 1717.

The fountain on Isola Bella, Lake Maggiore, Italy. Second half of the seventeenth century.

most extravagant point. In the Kaisersall of the Residenz at Wurzburg, for example, there is a splendid ceiling by Giovanni Battista Tiepolo, the greatest decorative artist of his time, in which the great painted centre-piece is surrounded by moulded and gilded decoration, in which the shell motif is treated with fantastic freedom. The same is true of the grand staircase in the same building, where colossal sculptured figures holding what one can only describe as disintegrated shells are interspersed with painted panels. Italian decoration showed a similar development. One of the most extraordinary examples of the use of shells is found in a fountain on Isola Bella in Lake Maggiore, a 'folly' of the most charming fantasy.

The shell was much used at the same period in the minor decorative arts all over Europe. We find shell-shaped snuff-boxes, bon-bon dishes in porcelain with a single scallop supported by dolphins or tritons; we frequently find that typical eighteenth-century contrivance the porcelain wall basin and cistern, the former in the shape of a shell, the latter sometimes decorated with shell motifs. Elaborate examples were produced at the porcelain factories of Dresden and elsewhere.

In England, under the Hanoverians, the shell continued to be used in the decoration of

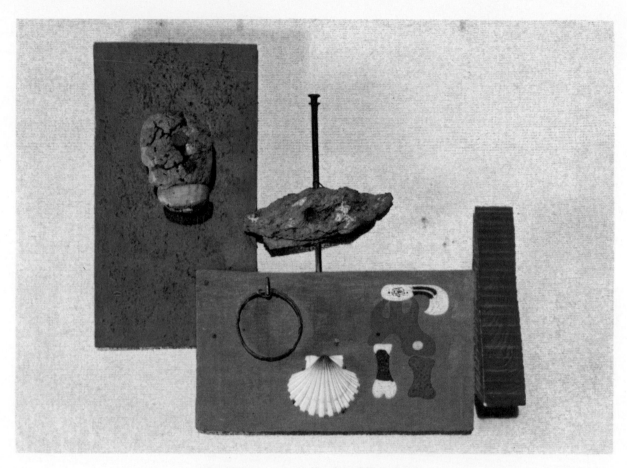

'Composition with Shell': Joan Miró, 1931.

furniture, notably on the cabriole legs of Chippendale chairs. It was also employed in elegant silver table dishes – stylized reproductions of the natural form of the shell without any decoration. When such an object was made on a small scale and provided with a handle it became that typically English thing, a tea-caddy spoon. Larger, and with a longer handle, it was transformed into a punch-ladle.

In furniture and interior decoration England avoided the rococo, but this does not mean that the shell fell out of use. Indeed, the enthusiasm of the English decorators for Palladio preserved it in a purer form. We find it used extensively by the Adam brothers in the plaster work of ceilings and as a dominant motif in their white marble chimney-pieces. That the shell-topped alcove persisted into the later Georgian period can be seen in the hall of Brocket Hall, Hertfordshire, a house begun about 1760 from the designs of James Paine. But towards the end of the century a severer neo-classical style prevailed and in this the shell motif found small place. It was crowded out by the trophies and sphinxes which were more to the taste of the 'Empire' designers in France and of the 'Regency' designers in England.

So far as the Regency was concerned, however, the shell staged a curious revenge, for if it passed out of formal decoration it reappeared in a fantastic form in what might be termed

'Pavilion' furniture. The Regent had a whole set of chairs and tables made entirely in the shell form, the seats of the chairs being one huge flat shell carved in wood and painted to represent the natural appearance of the scallop.

Perhaps this was a foretaste of the fate which was to befall the shell as a decorative motif in the nineteenth century. Obviously it could find no place in the Gothic revival, except perhaps, once more, as a religious symbol on the hat of a sculptured saint. But what we have called its 'Pavilion' aspect developed into a 'seaside' aspect. The early Victorians collected actual shells and decorated boxes with them or grouped them under glass shades. Shells decorated picture frames containing representations of the sea beating over the promenade. They passed into the 'Present from Brighton' category of 'popular art'.

Perhaps this seaside art may be said to have reached its apogee in the late eighteen-nineties and the early nineteen-hundreds. The sale catalogue of a firm in the City of London issued about this time lists an astonishing variety of objects decorated with shells. Describing themselves as 'Shell Merchants and Shell Manufacturers' the vendors offer to the public, at most reasonable prices, shell paper-weights, shell purses, shell brooches, shell hair-tidies, shell pincushions, shell mirrors, shell trinket-boxes, shell picture-frames, and even shell crucifixes and shell shrines. It is as if the shell were making one last bid to be the inevitable canopy over the head of a saint. Of course all kinds of shells were used, but the scallop was not forgotten and often formed the apex or the centrepiece of a shell composition.

So far as the use of the shell-motif in decorative art is concerned, this might be thought to be the end of the story, for the scallop found no place in the medieval revivalism of William Morris, in the kind of furniture and decoration beloved of the Æsthetes and in *Art Nouveau*. We look for it in vain among the austerities of modern decoration. But the shell has reappeared in modern painting, depicted for its own sake as a fascinating shape, as in the picture by Miro, reproduced on the previous page. If as a motif of decoration it seems, for the time at least, to have vanished completely, it may yet find a place in the decorative compositions of semi-abstract painters or the strange evocative visions of the surrealists. In these, perhaps, we may see again, through the haze of dream or nightmare, Venus rising from the sea.

ESCALLOPS

IN ARMORY

The Hon. Sir George Bellew

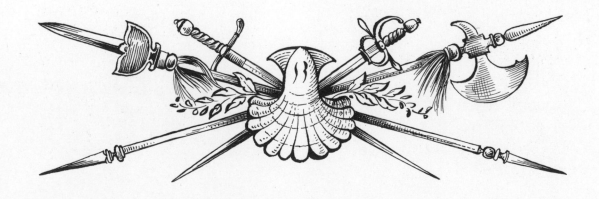

Illumination in a copy of Froissart's Chronicles including the arms of Philippe de Commynes, c.1450.

*E*SCALLOP shells occur in armorial bearings almost contemporaneously with the beginning of heraldry. The earliest known surviving examples appear on seals and in rolls of arms of seven or eight hundred years ago. Since then, down to the present day, they have occupied a consistently prominent place. In every hundred known English coats of arms approximately four have escallop shells as a principal part of their design. Though that may not seem a very high proportion, it should be remembered that there is an almost infinite variety of emblems and objects which can be used in heraldry, and of these some, like for example the pretty fleur-de-lis and the agrarian garb, or wheatsheaf, are as well favoured as the escallop shell, and a few, like the lion and varieties of the cross, even more so. Compare the popularity of the escallop shell with that of humbler shells, like the whelk, which appears but twice in every thousand arms.

Though examples of escallops in coats of arms occur as early as the mid-thirteenth century in written blazon, and these I shall mention again presently, perhaps the first, and certainly one of the first, to appear in painted records is a charmingly drawn shield of arms, containing a lion rampant and a scattering of escallop shells, which is depicted in a roll of the late thirteenth century in the College of Arms. It has no name to it but is of a pattern associated with a family of Hender of Cornwall. It is illustrated above.

Before I go on to describe the particular part played by escallop shells in heraldry it may perhaps be helpful briefly to explain the origin and essence of this 'little art and science'. Heraldry (or armory, as it is more exactly called) was in origin probably little more than a system of personal identification in warfare by means of distinctive patterns and forms displayed by leaders on their military accoutrements. It appeared in western Europe in about the middle of the twelfth century, and with a surprising suddenness, judging by contemporary evidences. It is, however, difficult to believe that it had not a formative period and perhaps even quite a long one.

Why heraldry appeared on the medieval scene so abruptly, and why indeed it appeared at all just at that particular moment in history, and apparently for the first time too, are questions still requiring definitive answers. It may, however, be supposed that certain novel circumstances, presumably of a military character, arose in or before the twelfth century in consequence of which a system of armory became desirable or perhaps necessary. Those

Above: Arms from a thirteenth-century manuscript.

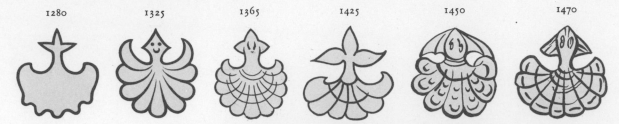

1280   1325   1365   1425   1450   1470

Forms of heraldic escallop, redrawn from old records. The dates are approximate.

circumstances may have had to do with the feudal system, or the crusades, or both, or with tournaments, or with something else. It is intriguing to speculate on this little problem and many have done so, but so far no unassailable conclusions have emerged.

Whatever the reasons were for the 'invention' of heraldry, and indeed some say seriously that it was an invention and that we owe the whole thing, or at least the initial idea, to some great forgotten inventor, there is no doubt that it soon became of remarkable importance in the medieval general scheme of things. Presumably this was due partly to its social significance, for it was closely identified with the aristocratic knightly caste, and partly to its peculiarly decorative qualities, which evidently appealed particularly to the medieval eye. We must also remember that a sort of aura of romantic symbolism grew up around it which was clearly very much to the taste of the people of those times, as indeed it has been to many ever since.

In early armory, understandably since it was a means of identification, two essentials were that every device used should be easily recognizable and that no device should be too like another. Distinctiveness in fact was a first consideration, and distinctive patterns and forms, which were often though by no means always the simplest, were therefore found to be the most useful. From this necessity for clearness and distinctiveness in design there emerged a novel and unique style of art. This was the style of the herald artist, or the herald painter, whose task it was to make indistinctive things distinct and distinctive things distincter. It was a style born of practical requirement, and it produced those patterns and forms, some grotesque, some of great charm, and nearly all distinctive, which have come generally to be known as 'heraldic'.

To illustrate this, let us take the heraldic lion. The king of beasts, if depicted as in nature, is not really a very distinctive object, especially when viewed at some distance or diminutively drawn. He could indeed easily be mistaken for some less noble beast. Therefore the herald painter contrived a lion which there could be no mistaking. This he achieved by emphasizing, or exaggerating, and perhaps in some ways beautifying, various points of the beast's anatomy. Thus the most telling lion, the ideal lion, in heraldry came to be one with jaws wide open, claws and paws of formidable proportions, an attenuated body which speaks of hunger and therefore fierceness, and an enormous, decorative tail. He does not perhaps look very much like a lion, yet it could well be said that he looks more like a lion than does

Forms of heraldic escallop, redrawn from old records and from life for comparison. The dates are approximate.

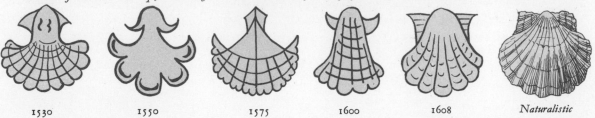

1530   1550   1575   1600   1608   *Naturalistic*

Pierced shell from an old grave, Holland.
Heraldic shell showing 'eyes'.

a lion in nature. To the medieval eye, at least, he clearly proclaimed his identity more efficiently than if he had been depicted photographically.

It is evident that the herald painter of old applied his art as best he could to almost everything he drew which he thought had need of it. When he came to that naturally beautiful object, the scallop shell, he must have judged that it required modification, if not improvement, for what he drew was not much like the scallop shell of nature. His interpretation of it was bolder, simpler, with fewer corrugations; and he introduced, presumably for added distinction, a deep notch on either side just below the 'hinge' such as no escallop shell nor indeed any other shell possessed. The result was pretty, shell-like, and certainly more distinctive than the natural thing. Not that all escallop shells, or indeed any other forms in heraldry, were or are drawn exactly alike: there has always been plenty of room for variations and artistic licence in heraldry. Certain it is, however, that the shells belonging to the first three hundred years or so of heraldry, that is to the period when heraldry had so much practical importance, were mostly drawn in the manner just described. Later, in the sixteenth century and after, when heraldry's original purpose was waning, and its uses changing, the escallop shell, like other heraldic forms, tended to become naturalistic. That was perhaps a pity, but changing times produce changing taste. In the last century taste almost wholly favoured naturalistic representation of all things in heraldry. In the present century there has been a swing the other way. But curiously enough this has not affected the escallop shell much and it is usually depicted now in heraldry more or less like it is in nature. The medieval heraldic pattern seems to have been overlooked in this return to simpler and bolder designs.

The escallop shell in heraldry is very nearly always depicted with the 'beak' uppermost. That is probably not because this happens to be its true morphic position in zoology, the hinge being at the top, but because it was commonly seen in that position, attached to the raiment of pilgrims, or perhaps hanging on the wall at home; it would indeed be awkward to hang it in any other way. Like the horseshoe and many other charges in heraldry, its normal position is the one in which you would normally see it. It is always possible, however, that it is shown as it is simply to distinguish it more easily from other things too like it. At all events, heraldry certainly took note at an early date of the manner in which scallop shells were attached to pilgrims' robes or elsewhere. In representations of the shell in old records of arms, particularly in those of the fifteenth century, we often see what look like two eyes in the 'beak' of the shell. These occur persistently enough to suggest that they were not there by chance. It can be assumed that they were in fact meant to be eyes, in the sense of holes, bored in the shell, through which a suitable thong could be passed for fastening. Examples of such shells have been found from to time; one from Holland is figured above.

Armorial seals: thirteenth and fourteenth centuries.

It is unlikely that the heraldic escallop was ever intended to represent any particular species of the genus *Pecten*. Such nice distinctions as are now made between, for example, *Pecten maximus* and *Pecten jacobaeus*, would be normally irrelevant in heraldry where, for better or for worse, an escallop is just an escallop and no more. The manner of depicting it there, however, was formerly so distinctive, and so unlike any of the known pectinids, that perhaps it should have had a special name in heraldry such as is sometimes given to other formalized objects. In ancient heraldic records it is sometimes called *coquille*, which is but the French for shell.

Gerard Legh, in his *Accedence of Armorie*, published in the sixteenth century, wrote of one of his subjects: 'He beareth Argent, iii Escaloppes Geules. This is a shelfishe, engendered of the Ayre, and dew. . . The shel thereof is the fairest instrument that can be, being of nature's making . . .' Though the author was evidently at sea in respect of the genetics of the pecten, no one will disagree with his assessment of the beauty of its 'shel'. He seems, however, to make a distinction between the 'escaloppe' and the 'shel', his words rather implying that it is the whole animal, both shells with the creature itself between them, that we see as a charge on a shield. In heraldry it is sometimes blazoned 'escallop' and sometimes 'escallop shell'. Nevertheless, since it is only one shell, and presumably the convex one, which we actually see, and since the pilgrim's scallop, so often used in heraldry, is unquestionably a shell, it is perhaps safe to declare for the shell and not for the mollusc entire. We should perhaps pause here to consider also the question of spelling. Should it be 'scallop' or 'escallop'? In written heraldic blazon it is usually the latter, but it is sometimes the former. The answer must be that in heraldry the words are synonymous and interchangeable like scutcheon and escutcheon, scroll and escroll, and doubtless several others.

The reasons why people chose particular designs and emblems and placed them for the first time in shields, which we can think of as, till then, undecorated, must have been many and various, and sometimes no doubt of the slenderest and most whimsical kind. We can imagine that many a design was chosen for no other reason than that it was distinctive. Even

Punning arms: Herringaud, Cockfield, and two families of Shelley.

Punning arms: Corbet, Arundel, Vavasour, and Scales.

though it meant nothing in particular it would in time come to be associated with the user and, eventually, with his descendants and family. The actual patterns and forms used were of all kinds, from crosses to checker-boards, from lions to butterflies, from horseshoes to escallop shells; some of them seem to derive from such ordinary things as simple decoration, the constructional parts of a shield, articles of clothing, and so on. Other reasons for adopting a particular design would be to express a worthy sentiment, to commemorate an event, or to proclaim feudal or family connexions.

Many designs of arms contain, by means of a pictograph or a kind of pictorial pun, an allusion to the bearer's name or to something else particularly associated with him which would help to identify him. Such arms are called by later writers canting or allusive arms. The clues contained in them are often very devious, and occasionally they are so recondite that their allusive elements take a great deal of finding. Such designs in heraldry have ever been popular and it is evident that the devisers of arms in the Middle Ages often went to extraordinary lengths to contrive them. Among this kind of design are such obvious allusions as herrings for Herringaud and cocks for Cockfield, escallop shells for Shelley, and whelk shells for another Shelley. Less apparent but still fairly obvious are crows (corbies) for Corbet, swallows (hirondelles) for Arundel, and a 'dance' (a design not unlike several letters V) for Vavasour. In the same category, but more obscure, are escallop shells for Lightfoot, Shank, and Scales (Professor Woledge in his chapter provides a clue to this last); and for Foljambe and Pateshulle (*pate* is akin to the Latin *patera*, meaning a shallow dish, and *shulle* is phonetically akin to *shell*). In the same way Cheyndut has an oak tree, and Swift a dolphin (noted in fact and fable for its swiftness); Montagu displays a pattern which looks like pointed mountains (*monts aigus*) and Stourton has fountains, said to represent the sources of the river Stour, from which his name derives. Ferrers has horseshoes, his ancestor being traditionally a farrier. Hakelut has axes. And Wauncey, seemingly not to be left out of this at any cost, has gloves which in Norman French were *gaunz*.

Punning arms: Shank, Foljambe, Lightfoot, and Pateshulle.

Ralph Bigot

Ralph FitzNichol

Martin Chamberlain

Geoffrey de Langley

Oted de Granson

William Dacre

Robert de Scales

Roger Prychard

William Tracy

Walter de Everley

Nicolas de Oddingselles

John de Uffard

Simon Crombe

John Danyell

Wat de Malecastre

Several users of escallop shell arms are noted in written records of the mid-thirteenth century. Ralph Bigot of Norfolk has a cross gules on a gold field with five silver escallops on the cross. Ralph FitzNichol has an 'orle' (an inner border) of silver escallop shells on a red field with a gold cinquefoil in the middle. And Martin Chamberlain has '*de goules à trois Escallops d'or*'. Ralph Bigot's pattern of five shells on a cross has always been a favourite design, belonging at various times to a number of different people and families according to the tinctures used. There would be little difficulty in listing a couple of dozen of these, which is not surprising when one considers that there are no less than seventy possible combinations of colours in a pattern such as this, using only the seven principal tinctures of heraldry. It is a well balanced and distinctive design, and that is perhaps enough in itself for it being so well liked. But heralds of a romantic or imaginative turn of mind might see in it an allusion to the crusades and to pilgrimages of long ago; and indeed that would be a reasonable explanation. Ralph FitzNichol's ring of shells could likewise refer to pilgrimage, or to St James, the patron saint of pilgrims, or to something of that nature. But it cannot be denied that we are in the dark and that it could equally well refer to many other things. And that applies also to the golden shells of Chamberlain. It is a pity, but it is a fact that the origin and meaning of the designs in ancient arms remain largely unknown.

In later thirteenth-century records we find other names. There is Geoffrey de Langley with a black fesse between three black escallops all on a silver field; and Oted de Granson with three gold escallops on a bend gules, the field being also gold. William Dacre has red with three escallops silver, and Robert de Scales the same but with six escallops. This Robert, in a rhyming list of the knights who were present at the siege of Caerlaverock in 1300, is described as

Robert de Scales, bel et gent,
Le ot rouge o cokilles de argent

which could be translated as 'Robert de Scales, handsome and amiable, bore red with silver shells'. Of about the same period is Roger Prychard of Standon, with the same arms as Langley but in different colours; William Tracy, with nine escallops; and Walter de Everley, Nicholas de Oddingselles, John de Ufford, Simon Crombe, and a number of others, all with escallop shells in various combinations of colours and arrangements. Though there is nothing in some of these arms to suggest any particular reason for their choice other than what has already been said above, we ought perhaps to notice Roger Prychard, who would surely not by accident have had something in his arms so hard to prise open as escallops; and Robert de Scales, whose escallops we have already noticed as giving a clue to his name. And on the same lines even the shells of Nicholas de Oddingselles give us food for thought.

A fine example of fifteenth-century escallop shell heraldry is provided by an enamelled metal stall plate of the arms of Sir John de Grailly, Knight of the Garter, which is in St George's Chapel, Windsor Castle. Each stall plate in St George's bears the arms of a Garter knight and there are over seven hundred of them, dating from about 1390 to the present day. They are in the nature of memorials, though in recent centuries they have been put up during the lifetime of each knight. Sir John's dates from about 1420, though he was a Knight of the

Arms and crest of Sir Thomas Shank:
from a manuscript c.1550.

Garter as early as 1348, being in fact a founder member of the noble order. The arms displayed upon it are of the same pretty pattern as those of Ralph Bigot which we have mentioned above, five escallops on a cross, the only difference being that Sir John's cross is black.

Sir John de Grailly came from the Bordeaux country, not far from Arcachon at the mouth of the Gironde, where he possessed a fortress by the seaside known as Buch. He was a man of considerable estate and had large interests in Bordeaux, and since that ancient city does, and apparently always has done, a thriving trade in scallops, one might be pardoned for thinking that Sir John's arms reflected an interest in the shell-fish industry. Though that might be so, we should perhaps also note that the heraldic form of escallop shell has an edge which in old heraldic blazon could be called 'engrailed', which means 'scalloped'. In French it would be *grêlé* which is phonetically akin to Grailly.

Arms and crest of Sir John de Grailly, Knight of the Garter: from his stall plate at Windsor.

There have been many other Knights of the Garter since who have borne escallops in their arms. Thomas Lord Scales, Sir John Fastolfe, Sir William Chamberlain, and Thomas Lord Dacre of Gillesland are names well known and honoured in English medieval history. Later there were the Russells, Dukes of Bedford, whose family provided many Garter knights, and the Villiers, whose arms were of the pattern of Ralph Bigot's: five escallops on a cross, gold on red on silver. Two Garter knights of recent creation are Sir Winston Churchill, with escallops in his quartering for Spencer, and Sir Anthony Eden with 'gules on a chevron argent between three garbs or banded vert as many escallops sable', arms which came to him from his ancestors of long ago.

Knights of the Garter: Sir John Fastolfe, Russell, Dukes of Bedford, Sir Winston Churchill, Sir Anthony Eden.

Badge of The Trustees for   Methodist Church Purposes.

Escallops are not confined to shields of arms only. They occur sometimes as crests (the devices worn on top of the helm in ancient times) and also as badges. There are today, in round figures, nine hundred English arms recorded in the College of Arms with escallop shells in them, ninety crests, and fifteen badges. One may well wonder why the escallop was so well liked, and why, for example, people continued to choose it as an emblem in their arms long after heraldry's functional use had declined and pilgrimages of the olden kind had

Escallops used in crests: Smyth, Lenacre, Wollmer, and Hopwood.

become a thing of the past. Perhaps it was done principally because men liked, as they still do, to remember the romantic past. In words ascribed to the physician, Thomas Fuller, who practised in Sevenoaks and died at the age of eighty in 1734:

> *The scallop shows a coat of arms,*
> *That, of the bearer's line,*
> *Some one in former days hath been*
> *To Santiago's shrine.*

Besides being a special emblem of pilgrims, the scallop shell is the well-known badge or cognizance of St James of Compostela, who in life was a fisherman and one of the twelve

Reading Abbey   St James the Greater

Arms and heraldic standard of Lord Dacre of Gillesland, c.1525.

apostles, and in death became the patron saint of Spain and of pilgrims. Presumably it was assigned to him because he had become, though long posthumously, the patron of pilgrims. The various legendary stories of how he came to adopt the escallop shell as his badge were probably devised later in order to explain the mystery. Christopher Hohler, in his contribution to this book, has considered the association of the scallop with St James in medieval art. This association has, however, an additional significance in heraldry because it was the custom, perhaps as early as the thirteenth century, to assign coats of arms posthumously to saints long dead, and indeed to other and even more important members of the celestial hierarchy. Such arms, to judge by surviving examples of them, were sometimes changed at will or invented anew, perhaps because they were not well known. Thus St James seems originally to have been given the simple arms 'azure three escallops or'; but we find also attributed to him, evidently in later times, other designs such as 'gules two pilgrims' staves in saltire or surmounted in the centre by an escallop argent', and 'argent a pilgrim's staff erect between a pilgrim's scrip and scallop proper', and again 'gules a cross potent between four escallops argent'. The arms of Reading Abbey were apparently derived from those of St James, being the same as his simple arms but with the escallops silver instead of gold. He was the Abbey's patron, his veritable hand being preserved there, the gift of King Henry I of England.

Arms more recently devised for St James

See of Compostela   *Kingdom of Galicia*   *St James of the Sword*

The medieval vogue for St James was centred round his shrine and supposed place of burial at Santiago de Compostela in Galicia, an ancient kingdom in northern Spain; and around its coasts scallop shells were, and still are, plentiful. Curiously enough, however, the arms of the kingdom of Galicia have no escallop shells; they consist (there are variations in detail) of a covered cup, which is perhaps intended for a chalice, since from chalice (or the Spanish *cáliz*) to Galicia is phonetically but a step. The arms of the city of Compostela are also devoid of escallops. But the See of Compostela has them, together with a sword of St James, in its arms.

St James had another cognizance which, at one time in the Middle Ages, seems to have been much associated with him. This was a pretty impress consisting of a sword of a particular form and a scallop shell. It is probable, however, that this was really the device of the knights of St James of the Sword, a military fraternity said to have been founded by Ferdinand II, King of Galicia and Leon, in about 1175.

Like the Knights Templars, and the Knights Hospitallers, such orders were dedicated to religious and various other worthy purposes. The order of St James of the Sword was a Spanish order dedicated to the protection of pilgrims who, journeying on their way to and from Compostela, were being molested by the Moors. It seems likely that they were also pledged to drive the Moors from Spain, a thing which, in fact, was not achieved for several hundred years. Their badge was the sword and shell device mentioned above. The sword was in the form of a decorative cross or, alternatively, it could be described as a cross in the form of a sword with decorative quillons and pommel; the decoration was of a particular pattern, the pommel being in the form of a reversed heart, like the spade of a playing card, and the ends of the quillons being in the form of fleurons. The position of the scallop shell varies, but as often as not it is placed over the blade just below the guard. The sword was always red, with the blood of the Moors, so it was said, and the scallop shell was sometimes white and sometimes gold.

There are other fraternities of knight and orders of chivalry who have used scallop shells

Collar of the Order of St Michael from a portrait of Louis XII, c.1500.

Wencelagh   *Hopwood*   *Otterborne*   *Chenai*

as a badge in various ways. There is the order of the Ship and Scallop Shell, for instance, which was founded by St Louis of France as a mark of royal favour and esteem; it is said that he conferred membership of the order on those who accompanied him on his pilgrimage to the Holy Land in 1248. Like the Templars and the Hospitallers and the Knights of St James, the order presumably had a distinctive badge, and presumably it would have consisted of a ship and a scallop shell. There is, too, the order of St James of Holland with its pretty ceremonial collar of scallop shells linked together. Another to use scallop shells were the Knights of St Michael, an order instituted by King Louis XI of France in 1469 'in honour of St Michael who always preserved his holy mount and never suffered it to be taken'. The shells in this case are usually represented with both valves, perhaps to distinguish them from St James's shells. It is not, however, altogether certain that they are, or at least were in origin, intended to be scallops; they sometimes look more like cockles; in ancient records they are usually called simply shells. Whether they were scallops or cockles the reason for using them, one may suppose, was because they were found aplenty on the shores of the 'holy mount'. But it is not improbable that they had some special significance as well, a significance known to King Louis and his knights but which has since been lost.

It is curious that heraldry does not seem to take much notice of the other principal symbolic connotation of the scallop shell, namely its association in classical mythology with the goddess of love and beauty, Venus. It was her shell because she was born of the sea, or 'foam-born' as it is prettily described in ancient literature, and was transported to the shore in a sea-shell which, considering its convenient shape and surpassing beauty, could hardly have been any other than a scallop shell. Renaissance artists, like Botticelli, showed that in their time the story had not been forgotten – but Sir Mortimer Wheeler and James Laver have already given their attention to this topic.

There are exceptions, however, to the herald's apparent indifference to this connotation of the shell. One is the 'Esquire's Badge', a device of some curiosity, which is depicted in

'Esquire's Badge'   *Crest of Fitz*

Gerard Legh's *Accedence of Armorie*, and which is therein inscribed 'a Sagittaire Geules, within an Escalop Argent set on his name or worde. This is the badge of an Esquire of England'. It is clearly of the genre of shells associated in ancient art with Venus, the 'beak' being downwards and the concave interior of the shell, unlike St James's shell, being presented to our view. Together with the centaur who, one may reasonably surmise, represents equitation, he being as it were to the manner born, the device speaks happily of the two arts in which no doubt all good young esquires of England were once proficient! Almost the same device, but in the form of a crest borne upon a wreath, was recorded in the seventeenth century to the family of Fitz of Devon.

Some designs in escallop shell heraldry stand out because they are either particularly pleasing or unusual. Among these are the arms of Wencelagh, Chenai, Otterborne, and Hopwood. Wencelagh's design of four shells in the form of a cross is surely one of the most beautiful of all arrangements. Chenai's three shells chained and stapled speak of thirsty pilgrims at a fountain, about which there must surely be some romantic tale to tell which is, alas, not told. Otterborne's barnyard cock perched on an escallop shell, which are arms anciently recorded in England, must have a story too; it is curious that this very design is also found in ancient arms in north-west Spain. Hopwood's pattern is a notable combination of richness and distinction.

On the fringes of heraldry proper there has always existed a class of device or sign which has heraldic characteristics but yet is not heraldry. The technical reasons for this do not matter here; it is enough to say that they are often used much in the same way as are true armorial bearings and, therefore, give our subject an additional contemporary significance. One well-known example is the badge of the Pilgrim Trust; another has provided the context for the present book.

AN EXCURSION

INTO THE AMERICAS

Adrian Digby

Chlamys nodosus inlaid with gold used as a pendant: Aztec civilization, Mexico.

*U*p to the time of Columbus, America was not just 3000 miles away from Europe – it was another world. It has been suggested many times, I know, that the ancient civilizations there may have had some earlier contact with Europe but there is no real evidence in support of this, or to contradict the view that the Continent was virtually isolated from the Old World from the time when the first Americans crossed the Behring Straits from Asia until the discoveries of Columbus and the conquests of Cortez and Pizarro.

Whichever of the civilizations of the Old World we study, we find influences constantly appearing from elsewhere, stimulating ideas, improving workmanship and modifying design. The development of no one of these people, therefore, can be considered as something that took place entirely in isolation, without any of the influences that do in fact form part of our own individual past and should, therefore, be generally within our own comprehension. When we look across to pre-Columbian America, however, we find a people whose last contact with the Old World antedated any way of life that could be called civilization. Here, then, is a place and a time where we can study a question of great fascination: the extent to which people of another world, but whose minds were presumably very like our own, differed in their reactions to the same situations, objects, and opportunities that we ourselves have experienced during the last 5000 years or so in Europe and Asia.

Such a study must begin by examining these reactions in relation to specific things that are common both to the early Americans and to our own forebears. The scallop shell is an ideal object for this purpose.

While most shells have been used throughout the world either for their intrinsic decorative qualities, for tools, or as raw materials, being cut up and ground down into pleasing shapes in no way connected with their original form, the scallop shell, by its very nature, has but limited utilitarian value. It is generally too thin and brittle to be ground down for use as a tool – Dr Rees has already drawn attention to this delicacy of its structure. The flutings also are a further hindrance. Except perhaps gastronomically, or as a container, there is little practical use for it. On the other hand the ears and the delicate fluting form a design, complete in itself, attractive, and incapable of radical change. It is this that has appealed so particularly to human kind in the Old World and, therefore, it is in this respect that we should examine it in relation to the ancient Americans – how they valued it and to what extent it entered into their symbolism.

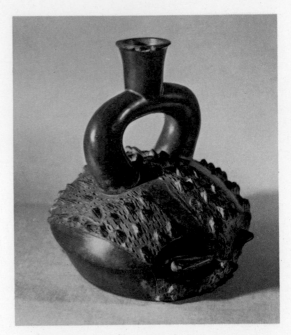

Pecten purpuratus worked by hand: Chile. c.3000 B.C.　　　*Vase with spondylus motif: Peru. c.900 B.C.*

In America, there is no doubt that the scallop was important, alongside other shell-fish, as an article of diet for the early coastal peoples, whether in California, or on the eastern seaboard of the United States or in the extreme south of the continent. In a number of widely separated places there are vast shell deposits, the natural rubbish heaps of fishing peoples who inhabited these sites for perhaps thousands of years. In these middens, the scallop is found with many other kinds of bivalves and gastropods, but not in a high enough proportion to indicate that the early Americans had any special fondness for it. In our understanding of these American coastal communities, however, we are limited by the lack of any ancient written language. Our only sources of information are the less perishable of the actual objects they used, the surroundings in which they are found, and, in the case of the higher civilizations, pictorial representations either in the round or as flat designs. To these we must add such relevant observations as the Spanish conquerors were able to record.

Perhaps the earliest example of American man's attempts to modify a pecten shell for his own use comes from the Taltal region of Chile, and was actually found in association with lance points and arrow points. It probably belonged to the later hunting peoples of about 3000 B.C. and is, in fact, of the species *purpuratus*. As the picture above shows, the edges have been ground away to make the outline as nearly circular as possible and the layer of purple near the lip, which overlaps the basic white of the shell and merges into it gradually, has been scraped away on its inner edge to leave a sharp dividing line between the purple and the white. It was probably used as a cup or drinking vessel, or possibly even as a lamp. However, so far as we know this treatment of a shell did not seem to have any universal application and, since it does not seem to have been repeated, we can assume that it was not regarded as a very successful venture.

Vases in the form of Pecten purpuratus: Mochica culture, Peru. c.A.D. 600.

After this age of hunters, there evolved in the Andean region a succession of more civilized and settled cultures, based on an elaborate agricultural economy and complicated irrigation systems. This lasted in one form or another down to the Spanish Conquest. A number of pottery vessels of this agricultural period bear witness to the continued interest of the South American Indians in the scallop, which, for our present purposes, I think we should take to include the spondylus – a member of the same family but, unlike the St James shell, biconvex and spiny. In the Museo Nacional in Lima there is a vase in which the body, lying on its side, is made to represent a large specimen of *Spondylus pictorum*. From the middle of one valve spring two spouts, trunked together like a stirrup for ease in pouring. This vase, which is illustrated on the opposite page, belongs to the Cupisnique culture of the northern coast of Peru which flourished roughly about 900 B.C. That interest in the scallop continued, we can see from two vessels of the Mochica culture, dating from about A.D.600, figured above. They are representations of *Pecten purpuratus*: one with a stirrup spout has the fluting of the original shell indicated by red painted lines, the other, slightly later in date, has a straight spout and is further of interest in showing the fluting by lines incised before firing.

The art styles and traditions of the Mochica passed on into the Chimu culture. From this there is the gold beaker illustrated on the following page. This has a band of unexciting and almost insignificant scallops as a minor decoration above the main element of the design which is a band of warriors clasping in each hand a shield and club, and with a mass of flaming, wavy hair. As the hair of American Indians is always long and straight, the wavy flame-like hair may well be attributes of the Sun God who, in a hot and arid region, would be regarded with fear and awe. The association with the shells, however, is so far without explanation. The same subdued treatment of the scallop is duplicated in the little stirrup

Gold beaker: Chimu culture, Peru.   *Pottery vase: Chimu culture, Peru.*

spouted vase of the same period illustrated above. The treatment of the shell itself is very similar in both cases. Radiating lines depict the fluting, and concentric arcs similar to those in heraldic devices in Europe suggest that a spondylus, or at any rate a rugged species of scallop (possibly *Chlamys nodosus*), was intended. But much more interesting are the two lugs or handles projecting from each side. They suggest a double outline like that depicted in English armorial designs of the sixteenth century. Compare them, for example, with Sir George Bellew's illustrations on page 92. The additional border may be the best approximation that a potter can make to the projecting spines of the spondylus, or it may be a convention to suggest an abundance of edible matter within the scallop. Also belonging to the Chimu period is a very interesting double vessel showing a spondylus shell joined to a beaker.

Three other vases from the Chimu culture, now in the British Museum, show the progressive conventionalization of the scallop motif when seen together as on the following pages. The first, in the form of a large spondylus or pecten shell standing upright on its hinges and with a flaring spout at the top, is not greatly conventionalized although there is a slight tendency to over-emphasize the scalloped edge of the shell. In the next example, a double vase consisting of a pecten shell on one side and a vulture-like bird seated on a crouching monkey on the other, the spines of the shell are indicated by irregularly overlapping triangles. The scalloped edge of the shell has become a series of deep serrations, or perhaps it would be more correct to call them cusps. In the third example illustrated here, the edge has developed into a wide band of pyramidal cusps, while the spines have become neat parallel rows of downward-pointing triangles. Neither the cusps nor the triangles have any direct resemblance to the parts of a scallop shell, though we can see that they clearly derive from such a source by looking at the intermediate stages of conventionalization when they are displayed in series as on pages 112–13. This last vase is interesting too in that the spout takes the form of a female human head, clearly shown by the long plaits descending on each side of the face. Who is this deity? We have no means of knowing. But she must be a goddess of the sea, the local counterpart of Aphrodite perhaps, or at least a goddess of shell-fish.

Let us now direct our attention northward, to the other great area of a relatively high civilization in pre-Columbian America: that which lies between the northern frontier of Mexico and Panama. Here there is rather more evidence of the use of the scallop and its near relatives. This is not surprising, because the region has been subject to more archaeological investigation than any other part of the Continent; for this reason also we know more about the Maya people who lived there than any other of the past civilizations of the New World.

In the Highlands of Mexico, a few miles north of the modern capital, lies the ancient ruined city of Teotihuacan. This was the leader of the so-called 'classic' cities of America, which reached their greatest activity between A.D.300 and A.D.900. Examples of Teotihuacan pottery have been found as far south as the Pacific slopes of Guatemala and there was a lively trade with the cities on the coast of the Gulf of Mexico. The Swedish archaeologist, Dr Linné, remarked that the inhabitants were evidently greatly interested in sea mollusca. On the walls of the temple of Quetzalcoatl, the feathered serpent god, bivalves and gastropods alternate below the undulating body of the snake, and on the pediment is carved an assorted heap of shells.

Further south, in Guatemala, British Honduras, and the south-eastern states of Mexico were the cities of the Maya, the Greeks of the New World, by whom the greatest advances in astronomy, in mathematics, and in the recording of time were made. They, too, knew and used the scallop. Examples of *Chlamys nodosus* and of a spondylus (both of them natives of the Pacific coast) have been found in graves and votive caches at many sites far inland, indeed almost all the way across to the Atlantic coast, in Mexico, Guatemala, and British Honduras. Many of these shells have been found perforated for suspension and were obviously used as ornaments; others contained small pieces of jade or cinnabar or pearl shell. There is, too, a Maya stela – a carved stone block – that shows a man actually wearing such shells suspended from a heavy necklace of jade beads.

In Maya symbolism shells are generally supposed to represent the earth. By implication, they stand also for the earth-monster and the abundance of the fruits of the earth. It is just possible that the symbol for the Maya day *Imix* may be a conventionalized shell (the day itself is presided over by the earth-monster) though it is more usually considered to represent a water lily. However, there is no doubt that shells of the scallop type were held in high regard by the Maya; this is evidenced by the positions in which they are found and the objects with which they are associated. They are, for example, clearly regarded as fit and proper surroundings for jade, the most sacred and precious material of that time and place – so precious was it in fact that a piece of jade was placed in the mouth of a corpse at burial to act as a talisman on the journey to the underworld. At Copan, a dedicatory cache under one of the stelae consisted of an assortment of jade and mercury surrounded by no less than thirty-eight scallop shells.

Progressive conventionalization of the shell motif in Chimu vases: I - Slight over-emphasis of the scalloped edge of the shell.

II - *The spines of the shell are shown by overlapping triangles; the figures represent a bird and a monkey.*

III - *The spines now shown as neat rows of triangles; the head of a deity forms the spout.*

In the burials the shells are associated with circular mosaic plaques made of pieces of iron pyrites. One example comes from a tomb of the early classic period (A.D.300–A.D.500) at Nebaj in the Peten district of Guatemala. This contained the remains of two adult males and three children, the latter probably sacrificed as attendants for the next world. The principal figure was found extended at full length on his back, with a mosaic plaque on each shoulder. Beside one corpse were the eroded fragments of two *Chlamys nodosus* shells, and beside the other there was one.

Also in Guatemala, at Kaminaljuyu, an adult male buried with three youthful attendants was found with three mosaic plaques, a pecten, and a spondylus shell. In this case, the body had been placed in a sitting position; but it had collapsed as it decayed with the result that the shells and the mosaics became mixed with the heap of bones and it is impossible to determine their original position. In another grave at Kaminaljuyu, probably rather earlier, an adult was buried full length with a pyrites mosaic on his stomach, and another on his knees. In this case, however, the plaque on his stomach had remained level and on it, still undisturbed, was a complete spondylus shell in which was a rough piece of unworked jade with some cinnabar. Pecten and spondylus shells have been found in association on other sites of Maya burials, and it seems inconceivable that the association was fortuitous. The use of the shell as a container for jade can be matched from Pusilha and other sites and, taken in conjunction with the votive cache from Copan, it clearly indicates the fitness in the mind of the Maya of these shells as receptacles for precious or sacred material – in these cases it was, perhaps, a special talisman or even the symbol of a god or goddess they contained.

It seems likely that, with the Maya, the mosaic plaque and the two halves of a pecten or a

Copy of a Maya wall-painting at Bonampak, near Guatemala City.

spondylus shell formed a single assembly, joined together with cord and possibly sealed with copal or some other adhesive – a somewhat cumbersome casket. The fact that the full complement of shells, two per plaque, is not always present can, I think, be accounted for by subsequent damage because in many of the graves in which scallops occur the shells have been almost completely destroyed by erosion. For the same reason, more examples of the thicker and tougher spondylus have survived than of the thinner and more brittle pecten.

Further light is shed on the intriguing problem of these shell caskets by the wall-paintings at Bonampak near Guatemala City. In one of these, part of which is reproduced above, fourteen distinguished-looking personages in white robes have assembled, apparently for instruction before taking part in a ceremony of some moment. Each of them wears three circular ornaments, of about the same size as the plaques, one on each shoulder and one on the chest. They have been described as shells by one authority and the outline of a shell can be seen on some of the discs in the artist's copy, but they obviously represent a complete assembly of mosaic plaque and scallop shell container with a piece of jade inside, exactly like the caskets in the graves at Kaminaljuyu. Surely these men must be priests in full regalia, wearing pieces of the sacred jade which gave them their supernatural authority.

The so-called 'classic' period of American archaeology ended somewhere round about A.D. 900, in turmoil and revolution. The priestly rulers were overthrown and, in many cases, the ancient cities were abandoned never to be occupied again. Teotihuacan was overwhelmed and a new phenomenon appeared in Central America: the warlike expansionist state. The people mainly responsible for this were the Toltecs from Tula, a city north of Teotihuacan. They extended their influence down to Panama and to Chichen Itza in far-away Yucatan. This revolution brought about the abandonment of many of the old conventions, and a

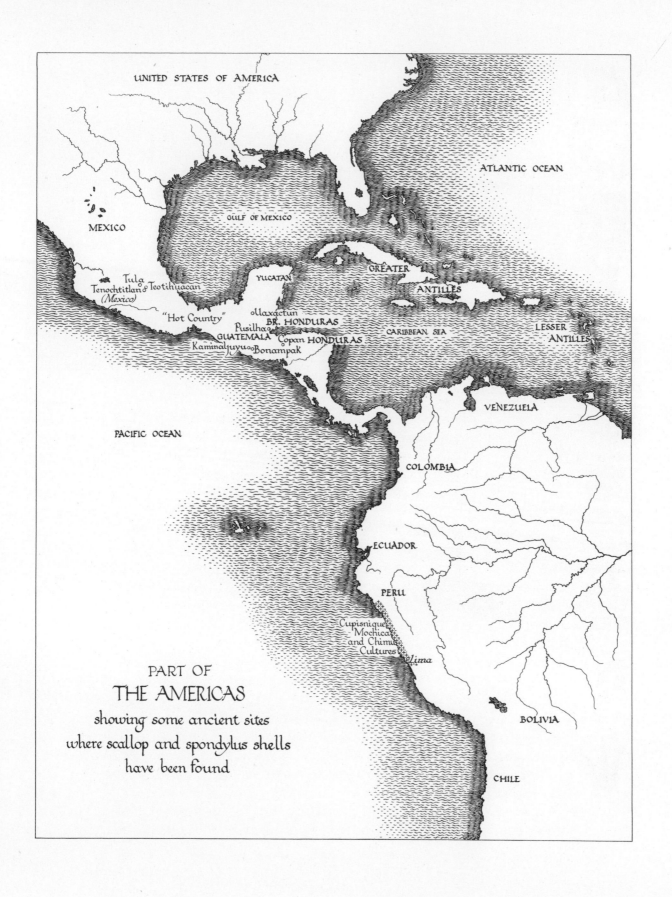

UNITED STATES OF AMERICA

ATLANTIC OCEAN

GULF OF MEXICO

MEXICO

YUCATAN

GREATER ANTILLES

Tula
Tenochtitlan & Teotihuacan
(Mexico)

Uaxactun

"Hot Country"

BR. HONDURAS

Pusilha

Copan HONDURAS

GUATEMALA

Kaminaljuyu

Bonampak

CARIBBEAN SEA

LESSER ANTILLES

VENEZUELA

PACIFIC OCEAN

COLOMBIA

ECUADOR

PERU

Cupisnique,
Mochica
and Chimu
Cultures

Lima

BOLIVIA

PART OF
THE AMERICAS
showing some ancient sites
where scallop and spondylus shells
have been found

CHILE

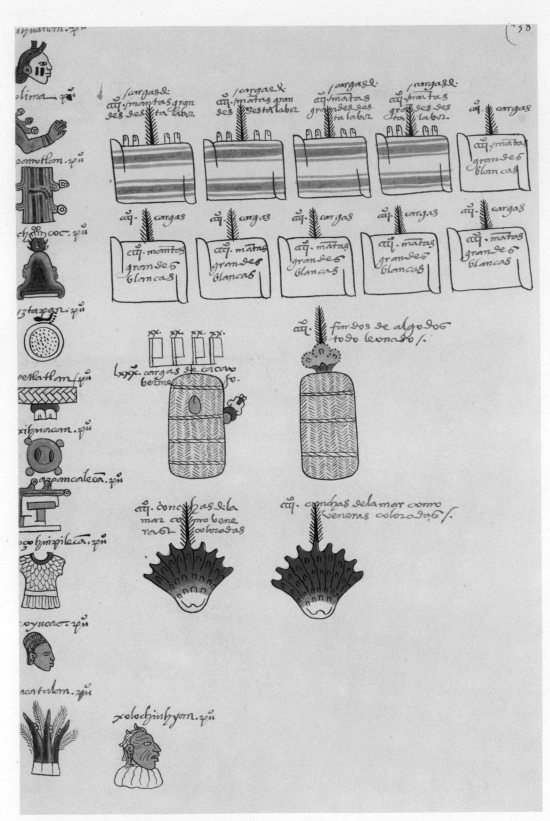

An Aztec picture manuscript: a page from the 'Codex Mendoza', mid-sixteenth century.

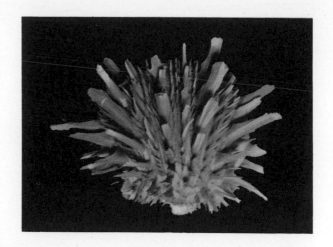

A modern Spondylus pictorum, for comparison with early American drawings and pottery.

change in the styles of art. The Toltecs do not seem to have carried on the use of the scallop to any great extent, indeed the only reference we have to it is on a fresco of the Casa de Barrios, where two priests worshipping the sun wear pendants to their robes which may well be pecten shells.

But in the remoter parts of Guatemala, Maya practices still survived in this 'post-classic' period, and in two cases burials at Zaculeu revealed scallop shells near the pelvis of the corpse. They may have been pendants worn round the neck, but a more likely explanation is to be found in the *Relacion de las Cosas de Yucatan*, written by Bishop Diego Landa in the year 1566, where he described the practice of girls wearing scallop shells as a pubic covering before marriage.

As time went on, the empire of the Toltecs broke up. In Yucatan the chiefs of the various cities waged bitter and treacherous wars against each other as did Alexander's satraps after his death, and in central Mexico wild tribes came in, settling in the lands of the Toltecs. One of these, the Aztecs, a humble nomadic group, settled on a marshy island near the shore of Lake Texcoco, gradually overcame their more civilized neighbours, and established a military empire, holding sway over and exacting tribute from the remnants of the Toltec domains. Among their tribute, due every six months from the vassal towns, was no less a number than 800 pecten shells. This was an astronomical figure when we remember how hard these shells are to collect; it may even explain their relative scarcity on those coasts today.

Details of this tribute can be found recorded in the *Codex Mendoza*, an Aztec pictographic manuscript with a contemporary Spanish commentary prepared to the order of the first Viceroy of New Spain, Don Antonio de Mendoza, and now in the Bodleian Library at Oxford. It is divided into three parts: a history of the Aztecs from the foundation of Tenochtitlan in A.D.1325 to the Spanish Conquest in 1521, a list of the tribute paid to Montezuma from some 400 towns, and an account of Aztec life from birth to death. It is only with the second part that we are concerned here. On one page listing the tribute from the 'hot country' cities, reproduced on the opposite page, the name glyphs of twelve cities are drawn down the left

117

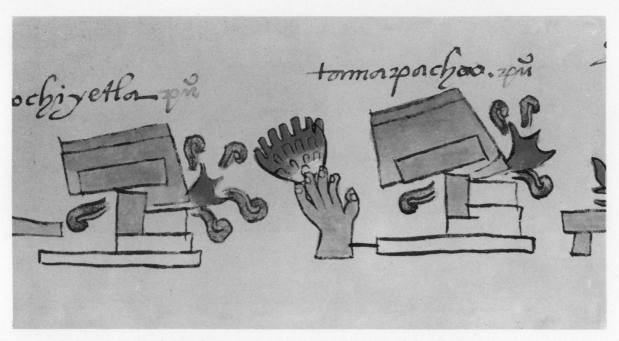

The sacking of the town Tamapachco: detail from the 'Codex Mendoza'.

side. The rest of the page is occupied by drawings of the commodities which were exacted from them: 1600 orange striped mantles, 2400 large white mantles, 80 bales of red cacao, 400 bales of cotton, and 800 red sea-shells, which appear to be spondylus. Some idea of Aztec numerals can be gleaned from the picture. Their system was vigesimal – based on twenties – and small multiples were represented by repetition. The Christmas-tree-like projections seen in the illustration are really plaits of hair symbolic of 400, and the four white flags over the bale of cacao each represent twenty, or eighty bales in all.

This is the only page in the *Codex Mendoza* showing shells, but even 800 seems a large number to import. They could not have represented shells containing edible fish; one trembles to contemplate the state they would have arrived in after a journey of several hundred miles on men's backs (the only transport available) in the tropics. What, then, were they used for? Spondylus has a comparatively thick shell and could, in fact, have provided the minute fragments of red in the predominantly turquoise mosaic ornaments and masks which were some of the most beautiful products of the Aztec lapidaries; but other scallops were undoubtedly used, with or without human modification, to serve as ornaments. A specimen in the British Museum, obviously intended as a pendant, was originally a *Chlamys nodosus*. The cusps which occur at intervals down the ribs have been broken off and filled with an inlay of gold foil, as is shown in the opening illustration of this chapter.

The only other occurrence of the shell in the *Codex Mendoza* is where a shell held in the hand is the name glyph for the town Tamapachco. This is illustrated above. The shell, the hand, and its position in the hand make up the complete name. This is derived from the three words *Tapachtli* (shell), *Maitl* (hand), *Co* (in). The pictures of a temple on fire, with the roof falling, is a graphic and vivid glyph meaning the sacking of the town. Altogether fourteen towns were sacked during the short five years reign of Tiçoçicatzin (1482–1486), which is recorded on the page of the *Codex* from which our illustration has been taken.

So much for the evidence. Now how are we to compare the ancient Americans' reactions to the scallop with those of their fellow men in the Old World? To take architecture first, there is obviously no close connexion. This is simply because they had no true vaulting, and no niches with hemispherical vaulting. The Americans, great though their architectural attainments were in many ways, never progressed beyond the corbelled, or false, arch made by cantilevering out large stones. They produced large flat rectangular surfaces far removed from the fan vaulting of Europe (which itself, no doubt, suggested the scallop as a decorative element) and contented themselves with decorative bands and unimaginative clusters such as those at Teotihuacan.

In ceramics and flat design, on the other hand, there is a relatively close comparison with Europe. The Americans in their representation of the shell, whether it be on Peruvian pottery or in the Mexican pictographs, offer examples of conventionalization and treatment of the shell which would not have discredited our own medieval heralds. In using it as the basic form for a pottery vase, even to moulding a goddess rising from the shell into a spout, the Peruvians were certainly at one in conception, if not in execution, with the Greeks.

Nowhere in America, however, do we find anything approaching a tradition based in the realistic portrayal of nature – especially of the human form – such as we in the Old World owe to ancient Greece. To the early Americans symbolism was everything. The female form was an emblem of fertility and its characteristics were emphasized so as to leave no doubt about it. There was no place in their worship for the charming, and often almost secular, poppets of the Greeks which Sir Mortimer Wheeler has described: their goddesses, like most of their gods, were more often formidable, or even terrifying, beings. Coatlicue, for example, the Aztec goddess of the earth (and thus, as a fertility goddess, in some respects the counterpart to Aphrodite) is shown in her best-known effigy as a being akin to the classical Medusa with two snakes for a head, a skirt of writhing snakes, and a necklace of severed hands. But she is cruder and harsher in feeling than Medusa by the very massiveness of her proportions. For her, birth from a dainty scallop would be unthinkable. On the other hand, on one of our vases, we have seen a Peruvian goddess arising like Venus from a shell, so we may be on firmer ground if we associate the Aztec goddess Chalchiuhtlicue with her, the clue being through the jade in the shell caskets of the Maya burials I have already described. Chalchiuhtlicue was the wife of the rain god Tlaloc, the goddess of the sea and lakes. She is sometimes known as 'She of the Skirt of Jade' and her special symbol, this jade, was carried (as we have seen) with cinnabar in the scallop shells worn by Maya priests and buried with them.

It would be tempting to see in this association of symbols an American version of the Venus legend of Europe. But we must be careful to separate fact from speculation. All we really know is that jade, the symbol of the goddess (and possibly regarded as something more – perhaps even the embryo of the goddess) was placed in the scallop with cinnabar, its red colour symbolic of blood, the food of the gods. Birth of the gods from shells was an idea familiar to the Central Americans, we know: Quetzalcoatl, for example, is often depicted emerging fully grown from a gastropod of uncertain species. But beyond this we cannot go. For one thing, there are many other reasons for the preciousness of jade: it was, for instance rare and beautiful; it was, too, the passport to the after-world. Either of these, or a host of other reasons we know nothing about, could explain the association of jade with the scallop. So, in the absence of any written language that could bring us into the minds of the ancient Americans, this particular association will have to remain a matter of speculation.

Admittedly, then, our evidence is slender; but there is, I think, enough of it to enable us to come to this conclusion: from the earliest times, and in isolation, the Americans derived very much the same sort of stimulation from the scallop as did their contemporaries in the Old World. The ways in which they expressed their feelings about it, however, differ, for they were conditioned (as one might expect) by the special character of their traditions and the different evolutionary pattern their various cultures followed.

THE SCALLOP AT

THE TABLE

Paul Gaultier – Sir Gavin de Beer

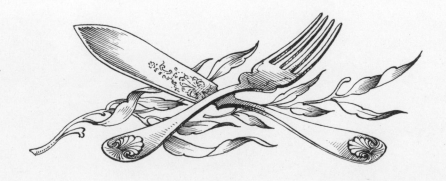

Scallops à la Nantaise

THE charmed name of '*Coquille St Jacques*' was given by the pilgrims in the Middle Ages to the scallop shell with which they decorated their mantles when journeying, as you have heard, to the tomb of St James at Santiago de Compostela. Clad in coarse cloth, staff in hand, they threaded their way on foot in long processions, praying and singing hymns, devoutly carrying their shells dedicated to St James, known in natural history as pectens or combs from the resemblance of their converging ridges to the high tortoise-shell combs worn by Spanish women in their hair.

> *Said she, then let us take*
> *Shell, rosary and staff*

scoffed Béranger as an invitation to the pilgrims to set out.

But as well as being the symbol of pilgrimage, that incomparable shell-fish, the scallop, has eminent historical, archaeological, aesthetic, zoological, and gastronomic qualities. All but the last have already received learned attention in the chapters that precede this: it remains for me to welcome the scallop, after its peregrinations through time and as far afield as the Americas, back to the table. In stressing its gastronomic qualities, I recall the memory of my friend Maurice Sailland, known by his wish as Curnonsky, acknowledged prince of gastronomers, who held in such high honour the delicious flesh of these molluscs.

Their plump bodies, white as mother of pearl, and their roes shaped like scarlet beans containing the eggs, when simply scalded or poached have a delicate taste of incomparable subtlety. As a treat they vie with lobster and particularly crawfish, which are tougher and rougher than the tender flesh fragrant with marine flavours that hides between the valves of a scallop, to the surprise and joy of gourmets. For this reason, no restaurant in Paris or the French provinces forgoes the honour of including on its menu scallops prepared according to its own recipe.

For there are thirty-six ways and a few more of preparing these succulent shell-fish by plain cooking if I may so express myself, making use of the thousand-and-one resources of the culinary art. I say art, for cooking is an art the secrets of which are precious for the health and joy of man, joy even of good fare producing good cheer and a proper balance of the faculties of body and soul, as evidenced by experts in good living. Blessed therefore be the scallops that allow our chefs and cooks, those venerated *cordons bleus*, jealous guardians of

Scallops en brochettes at the Italian table

our culinary traditions, to exercise their talents for the delight of connoisseurs. Not but that, if you should wish to savour scallops in all their impressive simplicity, I advise you to take your seat on a rough bench in some humble tavern of a fishing port in Brittany, facing the sun-speckled blue sea and to order scallops poached in their shells, cooked in butter and sprinkled with shallots and chopped parsley. The smart name for them would be *à la meunière*, as served fresh from Brittany in some Paris restaurants. Let us not forget that scallops are common round Mont St Michel, where pilgrims collected their shells to commemorate their visit; and has not Sir George Bellew told us of the Knights of St Michael who never suffered the Archangel's Mount to be taken, an order comparable with St James of the Sword in Spain? However these things may be, enjoy your plain scallops in peace, as is meet, washed down with white Muscadet, and, by my faith as a gastronomer, you will be delighted. You will become addicted to these famous shell-fish and their holy patrons.

How could the great chefs have failed to take advantage of the delicacies of such a mollusc to enrich their gastronomic palette? As you may imagine, they have not failed. They have laid under contribution all manner of wines, flavours, and aromas, in gustatory combinations more or less skilful, to exploit these exquisite shell-fish. As was natural, they began by the most complicated preparations. It is only after much hard work and perseverance that access is gained to that simplicity which is the summit of all art. What is true in literature, architecture, sculpture, painting, and music, also applies to cookery. The Parthenon, Berenice, Molière's *Le Misanthrope*, Beethoven's *Eroica*, *The Marriage of Figaro*, the *Venus de Milo*, *Mona Lisa*, are the achievement of supreme simplicity. All allowances made, the same is true of cookery. A dish that tastes of what it is and reinforces the flavour of those that accompany it is perfect, as our Curnonsky liked to say.

But perfection is not achieved all at once. It requires a great deal of time, work, experiment, patience, and taste, in cookery as in other fields. Beginnings are always difficult and therefore complicated. Scallops have been no exception. This is why, in the past, it was customary to surround them with all manner of culinary frills, mushrooms, truffles, tomatoes, ham, hard-boiled eggs, mussels, shrimps, pastry, and what not. Gouffe, a famous chef in the days of Napoleon III, indulged these fancies to his heart's desire. His principles were those of the bride-cake, works of architecture rather than of cookery, designed to please the eye more than the palate, highly esteemed during the second Empire and still in vogue in some palace hotels where the genuine taste of the products of nature is masked beneath compositions of artificial flavours.

Even closer to us, take the recipe that Escoffier gave for scallops *à la Parisienne*. He surrounds each shell with an unnecessary border of duchesse potatoes after having cooked the shell-fish in white wine with chopped truffles and mushrooms passed through melted butter,

Scallops en brochettes at the Italian table. With them are shown: Parma ham and melon; red mullet, prawns, and sea truffles; globe artichokes, fennel, pasta fettuccine, and Borlotti beans. The wines are Valpolicella and Soave Bianco from the Verona district.

the whole is covered with Duxelles sauce and ornamented with tomato *purée* and crushed shallots. This mixture is certainly pleasing to the palate but it emaciates the natural flavour of the scallop.

The same is true of scallops *Excelsior*, which are first boiled in brine, then in spiced white wine, and finally in hot milk. Meanwhile, mussels are set to cook, their juice is mixed with yolks of eggs and sharpened with lemon juice, and sliced mushrooms are added. This done, the shells are filled with equal quantities of the two preparations, and sprinkled with white bread-crumbs mixed with parmesan cheese before being put in a hot oven and then served well-browned. Would you not think that in this culinary combination the taste of the scallop disappears? How very much simpler, neater, and may we say more honest, are the modern recipes for scallops *à l'Americaine*, *à la Nantaise*, *à la Newburg*, or *au Champagne*, which have the merit of not masking nor obliterating, but of bringing out the taste of these delicious shell-fish, poached, sliced, or whole, and bathed in a fragrant sauce that would serve equally well for lobster or crawfish.

What could be more harmonious to the palate than the marriage of these sauces to the taste of the scallops which they strengthen without display or dressing. Like their clients, our modern chefs are not unappreciative of this gustatory harmony. They are none the less recipes of luxury against which I am glad to pit the simplicity of Nantes which I had the pleasure of enjoying one day in company with Aristide Briand, a great amateur of scallops as is proper for all Bretons. But listen. Here is the recipe for succulent shell-fish served to us in a small restaurant in Nantes, just as it was given to us with pleasure by the buxom proprietress. I transcribe it verbatim.

Scallops à la Nantaise

Obtain good shell-fish, remove the flesh and discard the black portions. Take two receptacles. In one place the white part and the roe, in the other the beards. Press the beards hard so as to extract the moisture, and slice them. Meanwhile melt some butter slowly in a saucepan with two minced onions, mix the hashed beards in with a wooden spoon and leave to simmer with a 'bouquet garni' of herbs and a clove of garlic for a good half hour. While this is cooking, cut the white parts into slices and place them in the preparation to cook slowly for a quarter of an hour. Take off the fire, add some crumbs of bread, butter, and a heaped tablespoonful of fresh-pounded parsley. Butter the empty shells, fill them three-quarters full and on each one put a piece of roe, a little grated bread-crumbs, and a piece of butter. Return to a very hot oven for five minutes and serve.

This meal washed down with a fairly sweet Breton cider was the occasion of a mercurial and dazzling conversation, as was usual on the part of Aristide Briand, of a depth and breadth of view characteristic of that great mind who not only understood but grasped the fundamentals of everything by rapid and profound intuition. This made him a master of that eloquence that moves and carries minds with it to the skies, full of a sympathy, a generosity, and an enthusiasm that belonged only to him. This will show you that my recollection of that dish of scallops is indelibly impressed on me.

It reminds me of another great man whom France lost much too young: André Tardieu.

Scallop bisque in the making. The other ingredients are John Dory, shrimps, Dublin Bay prawns; carrots, leeks, onions, and tomatoes for vegetable stock; spices, herbs, white wine, and cream.

The first lunch of the academy of gastronomers that Curnonsky had just founded on the lines of the Académie Française and, like it, containing forty members of whom André Tardieu was one, was held at a little old restaurant in the Saint André des Arts quarter of Paris, on the pavement where a long table had been laid. After the obligatory *hors d'œuvres*, the lunch began with a fine dish of scallops when, to the applause of the twenty-seven members, enlivened by a treacherous little Chablis, André Tardieu began to sing to give vent to his pleasure at this friendly gathering. What he sang was some verses in honour of the succulent dishes which followed on one another, of which scallops *à l'Americaine*, (that is to say cooked in butter, fired in lighted brandy, and anchored onto a basis of lobster *à l'Americaine* where they completed their cooking), had been prepared with a care which would have aroused the jealousy of the great Antonin Carême himself. Excited by a few bottles of Mumm *cordon rouge*, my friend's favourite wine, offset by an appetizing leg of venison *à la Grand' Veneur*, the twenty-seven companions struck up in chorus the song in which, as I have just related, scallops were not neglected.

Scallops at the Turkish table

THE SCALLOP AT THE TABLE

Nor were they forgotten at the table of that magnificent Amphitryon reincarnated in Camille Cerf, who every Saturday invited important figures in the worlds of science, letters, art, politics, finance, and industry, specially selected, to feasts of the most eclectic sumptuousness, enriched with the finest wines, feasts of which I fear the like will never be seen again. At these meals where the pick of Paris met under the title of *The Academy of Taste*, discussion ranged not only over topical questions of politics and art, but also of cookery. Our host's kitchen was in the charge of Madam Yvon, one of the most famous *cordons bleus* of the time. Among the guests were frequently to be seen Paul Reynaud, Emile Borel, Dumesnil, Professor Laubry, Raymond Poincaré, in a word, all that the Republic could show in the way of eminence. One of them had the duty of criticizing the meal, and that often fell to me, while another undertook its defence, under the chairmanship of the Grand Chamberlain, Heilbronner, Councillor of State, while the host with a kindly but sly expression looked on majestically from his seat. How often in front of this tribunal have I not had to sing the praises of the scallops, either in or out of their shells, which we had just eaten!

I say in or out of their shells, for there are two schools of thought, whether to serve scallops in sauce or in their shells. Many of my friends prefer the latter alternative as being more intimate and, shall we say, picturesque. These are the poets of gastronomy who appreciate a dish with all the more relish when their imagination plays on its origin; in the case of scallops for instance, the sea bottom which was their home.

In this connexion, I remember that I once praised the merits of scallops under quite exceptional conditions at Arlon in Belgium, at a private dinner given by Camille Cerf to his friends to celebrate his collar of *Commandeur* of the Legion of Honour. I remember this all the more vividly because by the fault of an unusual abundance of jeroboams the guests, who included a high dignitary of a sovereign court whom I was obliged to see home, fell asleep in their cups, as De Flers and Caillavet would have said. For scallops stimulate thirst in the palate, even when they have not been sharpened with spices. If they are best suited with Muscadet, they do not despise Chablis or the pale wines of Lorraine and Alsace, although on great occasions they prefer a proud Meursault or a powerful Montrachet, white of course, or even a vintage champagne. Who likes scallops likes wine, but in reason and with taste, in accordance with their delicate and variegated flavour.

By reason of their qualities, scallops play an important and well-deserved part in the composition of sea-pie, in company with mussels, prawns, crabs, and lobsters. They blend admirably with the various marine aromas which perfume this gustatory concert. In fact, the scallop although plebeian to the point of appearing on the mantles not only of pilgrims but of beggars, who for that reason are known as *coquillards*, is really aristocratic. Even if it likes

Scallops at the Turkish table: a shell-fish pilau including also prawns and ink-fish with saffron rice. The side dishes contain vine leaves stuffed with rice, black and green olives, scallops and taramasalata, aubergine and tomato, and leeks stewed in oil. The white cups contain sherbet and the pitcher and bowl are for rosewater.

simplicity, it is no less fond of luxury as witness certain recipes in which it delights. Consider for instance scallops *à la Newburg*. What richer or more refined dish could be set before even the most exacting, be they members of the *Club des Cent* or of the *Académie des Gastronomes*, where the art of good eating is esteemed and practised as a matter of first importance. I scarcely dare reveal to you the composition of this masterpiece of gormandize, so great will be your haste to want to taste a dish so fit for the gods, as used to be said by Brillat-Savarin, whose works and memory we venerate. But look:

Scallops à la Newburg

Extract the flesh from several scallops, cook them in a boiling liquor of wine with bay leaves, fine herbs, salt, and pepper, and then heat them with butter in a shallow pan. Add brandy and madeira, leave them to simmer for a few moments, and cover with thick cream, salted and peppered. Thicken by reducing slowly, and at the last moment pour into the pan a mixture of yolk of two eggs and a little cream. Do not allow to boil. Serve.

If you want to treat a V.I.P. from whom you expect some favour, if he is capable of appreciating good food, I advise you to offer him this dish in a big restaurant at lunch, well served on elegant crockery, the table covered with flowers. Before the scallops, drink a deceitful little wine from the Charentes, which combines the qualities of white wine from which brandy is made, with those of a slightly sweetened liqueur brandy, than which nothing is more appropriate to warm the cockles of the heart and whet the appetite. Follow the scallops *à la Newburg* with a well-grown pheasant stuffed with truffles *à l'ancienne*, as this dish is now called because of the infrequency with which it is seen today owing to questions of economy. After a fresh green salad served separately in accordance with the advice of Brillat-Savarin, re-appetize your guest with a fat Camembert just ripe, and finish with a pineapple ice which will refresh both your palates. From the start of your meal drink a Pommery-Greno, one of the kings of champagne, of a good year, but accompany the cheese with a generous and majestic Haut-Brion. After coffee, offer your companion who has by now become your accomplice an old and genuine Armagnac, reserved for none but the very greatest occasions. There is no finer bouquet for scallops. If after such a meal your lucky guest does not grant you his favour, by my faith as a gastronomer I shall never dare predict anything again.

In fact there is nothing like good eating to promote the unity of man. That is why at the present time there are so many groups and clubs where are celebrated the rites of good eating, an expression which I prefer to the pedantic word gastronomy. It is enough for me to quote the *Club des Cent*, the *Compagnons de la Bonne Table*, the *Psychologues du Goût*, the *Gastronomes régionalistes*, the *Grand Perdreau*, the *Gourmettes*, and the *Académie des Gastronomes* over which I preside. I cannot enumerate them all, for they are too numerous, to the joy of our fellow citizens. I need not tell you that all are faithful to the cult of the scallop.

This cult is so to speak universal. Under one name or another the scallop is esteemed in all countries with a seaboard whence it can be obtained. So the English delight in scallops which they prepare in several different ways, while the Japanese eat them raw, Americans use them for cocktails like crabs and lobsters, Spaniards dress them with green, red, and yellow pimento, the Portuguese eat them with a sauce *au vin blanc*, Italians fry them, Canadians sharpen them with paprika, Turks serve them cold with garlic mayonnaise, the Vietnamese reduce them to a fragrant mince, and Hindus mix them with rice. In passing we may note that these last possess the finest scallops, obtained from the Indian Ocean and known as *manteau ducal* or *Chlamys pallium*. These shells are the most elegant of all with their twelve convergent ribs, bristling with spines, and embellished by the harmonious distribution of white splashes against a variegated red background with brown mottling.

Our motley European scallop shell with rounded ribs (*Pecten maximus*) is the most common on Atlantic coasts. Their plump flesh, which is the edible part, is composed of the muscle by means of which they bring the two valves of the shell violently together, and thereby propel themselves with such power and strange precision through and in the water. Hunters, we are told, develop a curious affection for the quarry they needs must stalk, an emotion born of the understanding that comes from age-long observation of its nature and its way of life. Nor is the gastronomer impervious to such a quickening of his sympathy when, although denied the advantage of a bathyscope, he hears of the moving performance of the scallop in the words of such an observer as Philip Henry Gosse. Dr Rees has my gratitude for recalling them and Dr Wilson my wonder at the artistry with which he has captured this scene and preserved it so that all of us can be witnesses. Patrons of pilgrimage, then, scallops can travel to such good effect that on our coasts they disappear in April and take refuge in the depths against the heat of summer, to reappear in September.

All Honour to Scallops!

If I dared, I should propose for their devotees a banquet composed exclusively of these tasty shell-fish. I should begin with a scallop cocktail, highly spiced, followed by a sea-pie in which scallops would predominate. After this I should offer an entrée of scallops *au champagne* with which the guests could lick their chops, and follow it as a roast with sliced scallops spitted between rashers of bacon roasted on charcoal, in the manner in which M. Barnagaud has recently suggested. Scallop fritters would provide the dessert.

I present this idea to all devotees of scallops. Let those who like them follow me. It would be difficult to accord them too much honour, because as a talisman like St Christopher, who was a companion of St James the Greater, they are the patrons of the most popular and itinerant piety: the piety which led innumerable pilgrims and still leads them, albeit in automobiles, towards the tomb of St James the Greater who was one of Our Lord's favourite disciples. Scallops recall all these worthy memories to those who appreciate the pleasant taste of their flesh. They associate with it the beauty of their shells which have served as an inspiration to architects, sculptors, and painters from the beginning up to the present day.

LIST OF ILLUSTRATIONS

Shell: A Word's Pedigree

The Living Scallop

A Symbol in Ancient Times

LIST OF ILLUSTRATIONS

The Badge of St James

The Cradle of Venus

Escallops in Armoury

An Excursion into the Americas

The Scallop at the Table

Key to shells displayed on back endpaper

Equichlamys bifrons   12
New South Wales

Chlamys nobilis   13
Japan

Pecten (Euvola) ziczac   14
North Carolina to West Indies

Chlamys swifti   15
Japan

Chlamys lischkeri   16
Patagonia

Chlamys (Nodipecten) nodosus   17
South East United States and Caribbean

Comptopallium radula   18
Japan

Chlamys ventricosus   19
Peru and Ecuador

Notovola fumata   20
New South Wales

Chlamys opercularis   21
Atlantic coast of Europe

Pecten vogdesi   22
California